W9-CPE-830

Eddie Murphy

ACTOR

Black Americans of Achievement

LEGACY EDITION

Muhammad Ali

Maya Angelou

Louis Armstrong

Josephine Baker

George Washington Carver

Ray Charles

Johnnie Cochran

Bill Cosby

Frederick Douglass

W.E.B. Du Bois

Jamie Foxx

Aretha Franklin

Marcus Garvey

Savion Glover

Alex Haley

Jimi Hendrix

Gregory Hines

Billie Holiday

Langston Hughes

Jesse Jackson

Magic Johnson

Scott Joplin

Coretta Scott King

Martin Luther King Jr.

Spike Lee

Malcolm X

Bob Marley

Thurgood Marshall

Eddie Murphy

Barack Obama

Jesse Owens

Rosa Parks

Colin Powell

Condoleezza Rice

Paul Robeson

Chris Rock

Al Sharpton

Will Smith

Clarence Thomas

Sojourner Truth

Harriet Tubman

Nat Turner

Madam C.J. Walker

Booker T. Washington

Oprah Winfrey

Stevie Wonder

Tiger Woods

Black Americans of Achievement

LEGACY EDITION

Eddie Murphy

ACTOR

Hal Marcovitz

CHELSEA HOUSE
An Infobase Learning Company

Eddie Murphy

Copyright © 2011 by Infobase Learning

Chelsea House
An imprint of Infobase Learning
132 West 31st Street
New York, NY 10001

Library of Congress Cataloging-in-Publication Data

Marcovitz, Hal.
Eddie Murphy: actor / by Hal Marcovitz. — Black Americans of achievement, legacy edition
  p.   cm.
Includes bibliographical references and index.
ISBN 978-1-60413-844-3 (hardcover)
1. Murphy, Eddie, 1961–   —Juvenile literature. 2. Actors—United States—Biography—
Juvenile literature. 3. Entertainers—United States—Biography—Juvenile literature.
4. African American entertainers—Biography—Juvenile literature. I. Title.
PN2287.M815M37 2011
791.430'28092—dc22 [B]   2010026883

Text design by Keith Trego
Cover design by Keith Trego
Composition by Keith Trego
Cover printed by Bang Printing, Brainerd, MN
Book printed and bound by Bang Printing, Brainerd, MN
Date printed: January 2011
Printed in the United States of America

10 9 8 7 6 5 4 3 2 1

This book is printed on acid-free paper.

All links and Web addresses were checked and verified to be correct at the time of publication. Because of the dynamic nature of the Web, some addresses and links may have changed since publication and may no longer be valid.

Contents

The Making of a Movie Star

In the early 1980s, soon after Eddie Murphy emerged as a star on the TV sketch-comedy *Saturday Night Live*, his managers, Robert Wachs and Richard Tienken, started looking for a film role that would fit their client's talents. They were well aware of the career trap that often swallows up TV stars, particularly comics, who try to make a splash in Hollywood only to find that movie audiences often do not appreciate them when they step out of their familiar TV roles.

Some of the TV stars—dramatic actors and comedians—who have made largely unsuccessful transitions to the big screen are Roseanne Barr from *Roseanne*, Shelley Long from *Cheers*, Tom Selleck from *Magnum P.I.*, Matt LeBlanc from *Friends*, and David Caruso from *NYPD Blue*. Murphy's managers knew they were asking a lot. At the time, there were few African-American actors who could command star billing. For that reason, they knew they would have to pair Murphy with an established white star, but they also did not want him cast as a sidekick. After sifting through several projects, Wachs and Tienken knew they had found the right vehicle for Murphy in *48 Hrs.*

The movie tells the story of tough San Francisco cop Jack Cates, played by veteran actor Nick Nolte, who gets wisecracking thief Reggie Hammond released from prison for two days so Hammond can help him track down a killer. To play Hammond, Murphy would not be required to do much more than play the same type of character he played on *SNL*—a streetwise hustler willing to make fun of anyone to get a laugh.

FUNNY GUY, TOUGH GUY

The 1982 film *48 Hrs.* was produced by Paramount Pictures, a studio where many executives harbored misgivings about casting Murphy in the role of Reggie Hammond. The role had originally been written for Richard Pryor, then one of the leading black comedians in America. Pryor had achieved success in movies mostly by teaming up with his good friend Gene Wilder, a white comedian with whom he had forged a successful formula: Wilder always played the decidedly unhip bumbler while Pryor took the role of the street-smart hustler. When faced with danger, Pryor's character usually tried to joke his way out of the jam.

Although Murphy greatly respected Pryor, Murphy did not see his role as Hammond developing the same way Pryor would have played it. Murphy wanted the character to be funny, but he also wanted Hammond to be as tough as Nolte's character—a trait he displayed in what is perhaps the movie's most important scene: The trail has led Cates and Hammond to a country-and-western bar. Hammond assures Cates that he can squeeze information out of the tough-looking customers inside. Cates is dubious but gives Hammond the chance. The jiving Hammond, impersonating a police officer, struts into the bar and intimidates the stunned white customers,

Eddie Murphy, then a rising star best known for his work on the television sketch-comedy program *Saturday Night Live*, broke into movies with his role as fast-talking Reggie Hammond in *48 Hrs.*, a 1982 film directed by Walter Hill and costarring Nick Nolte.

making them divulge all they know. In the most dramatic moment in the scene, as recalled by Patrick McGilligan in "Walter Hill: The Last Man Standing" for *Film Journal International,* Hammond scowls at one of them and says, "I'm your worst . . . nightmare."

Walter Hill, the film's director and cowriter, said that scene was rewritten several times before the writers convinced themselves that the audience would believe a skinny African-American con man could intimidate a bar full of brawny, bigoted whites. "[We] were rewriting Eddie to the very last day of shooting," Hill recalled to McGilligan. "The more we learned, the better we got. Of course, it's obvious that he was a gold mine of talent. I guess we did something right—Eddie played basically the same character for the next 10 years."

CONNECTING WITH WHITE AUDIENCES

Each day after shooting, Hill would send the day's "rushes" to Paramount headquarters in Los Angeles where the company's executives could follow the progress of the movie. (Rushes are the scenes shot each day—they are composed of the raw, unedited footage of the actors playing their roles.) Soon after they saw the rushes that included Murphy's scenes, particularly the scene in the bar, the Paramount executives wondered whether Murphy could connect with the mostly white audience members they expected to buy tickets to the film.

So they summoned the director to Los Angeles and urged Hill to fire Murphy and recast the part of Reggie Hammond. "They didn't think he was funny," Hill said, as quoted by Josh Rottenberg, Vanessa Juarez, and Adam B. Vary in "How Eddie Got His Groove Back" for *Entertainment Weekly*. "He wasn't giving a broad comedic performance. They wanted somebody who would do it like Richard [Pryor]. Eddie was different."

Hill refused to fire his star, then he left Los Angeles and returned to shooting scenes for the film in San Francisco. Back at Paramount, the executives debated among themselves and—finally and reluctantly—gave Hill permission to continue shooting the film with Murphy in the role of Hammond.

BLOCKBUSTER HIT

Back in San Francisco, Murphy was harboring his own doubts about the movie. Because he was still a member of the *SNL* cast, the TV comic actually showed up on the set a few weeks after filming had commenced. Murphy was obligated to finish the 1981–1982 *SNL* season in New York before he could join the movie production on location, across the country in California. After arriving on the set, Murphy seemed to everyone to be the same cocky and self-assured wiseguy that TV audiences had come to love. Inside, though, he was full of self-doubt. Murphy had never acted in a movie before and soon realized that he did not know the first thing about film acting.

For starters, the film was shot out of continuity, meaning that scenes that appeared late in the film were shot early in the production schedule. Veteran actors are used to dealing with shooting scenes out of continuity—they study the script and spend time preparing themselves for the scenes—but Murphy found himself confused by all the skipping around. Later, he recalled, as quoted by Frank Sanello in *Eddie Murphy: The Life and Times of a Comic on the Edge*:

> I called my manager and said, "My career is ruined. It's over. I'm twenty-one and I'm all washed up." I didn't know what a reaction shot was, and I'd never filmed anything out of continuity, so every morning Nick [Nolte] had to tell me where we were in the story and how the characters were supposed to be getting along.

Despite Murphy's doubts, Hill was delighted with the work he was getting out of the comic. Murphy proved himself quite capable of sharing scenes with Nolte. He was not intimidated by the veteran actor, bringing enough swagger and self-confidence to the role of Hammond to make audiences believe he truly was the jiving character he portrayed.

Movie critics regard the scene in the bar as an example of Murphy's best work in film. "Murphy has a sneaky genius for getting audiences on his wavelength," wrote *Texas Monthly* film critic James Wolcott, "and in the scene in which he shakes down a redneck bar, he so brilliantly turns the audience into co-conspirators that we seem to be up there on the screen with him, egging him on to more daring mischief." Another film critic, Roger Ebert of the *Chicago Sun-Times*, remarked:

Sometimes an actor becomes a star in just one scene. Jack Nicholson did it in *Easy Rider*, wearing the football helmet on the back of the motorcycle. It happened to Faye Dunaway when she looked sleepily out of a screen window at Warren Beatty in *Bonnie and Clyde*. And in *48 Hrs.*, it happens to Eddie Murphy.

48 Hrs. opened in theaters in late 1982. The movie received strong reviews and also turned out to be a blockbuster hit at the box office, grossing nearly $80 million in ticket sales. The film would even spawn a sequel—*Another 48 Hrs.* By the time that movie (again starring Nolte and Murphy) was made eight years later, Murphy had established himself as one of the most popular and bankable movie stars in Hollywood.

2

Born to Be a Comic

Every afternoon as a child, Eddie Murphy and his friends rushed home from school, finished their homework quickly in the Murphy family kitchen, then watched their favorite situation comedies, which included *All in the Family*, *Good Times*, and *The Honeymooners*. *All in the Family* featured an African-American character, George Jefferson, who was played by Sherman Hemsley. Jefferson was a proud black man who took no guff from the show's main character, the bigoted white loading-dock foreman, Archie Bunker. When Jefferson insulted Bunker by snapping, "Your mama!" Murphy and his friends exploded in laughter.

Soon, Eddie and the others used that line whenever possible, always with the intent of getting laughs. Murphy's childhood friend Harris Haith recalled in his book *Growing Up Laughing with Eddie Murphy*, "It was the greatest thing we ever heard because we said, 'Hey, this guy acts just like us,' and 'He's crazy, just like us.' We would not hesitate to talk about someone's mother or father or any family relative if we thought we could get a laugh out of it."

Of course, nobody in Eddie's circle of friends could get laughs the way he could. He was constantly making jokes, imitating celebrities or teachers, and finding other ways to get laughs. "The truth is, I knew what I was put here to do," Murphy said years later to David Rensen in a *Playboy* interview. "Until I was 10, I wanted to own a Mister Softee ice cream truck. But after that, I knew I wanted to be in show business."

LIFE IN ROOSEVELT

Edward Regan Murphy was born April 3, 1961, in the Bushwick section of Brooklyn, New York. At the time of his birth, Bushwick was a low-income neighborhood. Many people who lived in Bushwick were unemployed and crime and drug use were rampant. The Murphy family lived in public housing,

IN HIS OWN WORDS . . .

Eddie Murphy says he gets a personal high out of making people laugh. He likens the high to the euphoria felt by drug abusers. Murphy once said:

It's like medicine. Used to be, if I was depressed, I'd just go somewhere and do a show and try to work really hard, and they clap at the end, and you feel yourself worth it again. Now I just walk into a club and people start clapping. I feel like saying, "Thanks, I was really depressed, but I'm not now, so I'm leaving. . . ."

I'm not the Savior. I'm just a brother that God happened to give a little talent to, and I just happened to luck out and get into show business, and I tell jokes, and if they get laughs, fine, and if they don't get laughs, fine, I'll work it out.*

* Joseph Dalton and David Hirshey, "Eddie Murphy: The Prince of Comedy," *Rolling Stone*, July 7, 1983, p. 19.

Growing up, one of Eddie Murphy's favorite television shows was *All in the Family*, an Emmy award-winning sitcom that ran on CBS from 1971 to 1979. His favorite character was the African-American businessman George Jefferson, played by Sherman Hemsley, who often sparred with his bigoted neighbor Archie Bunker, played by Carroll O'Connor.

meaning that a government agency built their apartment complex and paid part of their rent.

Bushwick is the type of neighborhood that has spawned many black entertainers, particularly comedians, who manage to find humor in their troubled upbringings. Murphy's future idol, Richard Pryor, grew up in a slum of Peoria, Illinois, and often joked about his early life on the streets. Before Pryor rose to stardom, Bill Cosby told many jokes about growing up in his tough Philadelphia neighborhood.

For Murphy, however, his early life in Bushwick would not serve as an inspiration for his later work on stage. Murphy's parents, Charles and Lillian, divorced when he was three. Murphy did not have much of a relationship with his biological father; when Murphy was eight, Charles Murphy was stabbed to death by a girlfriend. By then, Lillian had remarried, and Murphy's stepfather, Vernon Lynch, soon moved the family—Eddie, as well as older brother Charles and younger brother Vernon—to the largely black suburban community of Roosevelt on Long Island. "We never wanted to go backward," Vernon Lynch said, as quoted by Joseph Dalton and David Hirshey in "Eddie Murphy: The Prince of Comedy" for *Rolling Stone*. "We always wanted to go forward. Eddie never knew anything about [the] ghetto."

In Roosevelt, the family lived in a comfortable house in a lower-middle-class neighborhood. Lillian and Vernon both had jobs—Eddie's mother worked as a telephone operator while Lynch worked as a foreman in an ice cream factory. Lynch was very serious about schoolwork—he wanted the boys to go to college and find good careers. He worked the night shift at the factory, arriving home when Eddie and his brothers were just getting up for school. "I wanted those boys up and out, working or at school," Lynch said to Dalton and Hirshey. "Got to get going. Got to hit the street."

QUICK WITH AN INSULT

As Vernon and Lillian Lynch soon realized, though, Eddie had very little interest in schoolwork. At school, Eddie carried a C-minus average. Likewise, he was hardly a skilled athlete. He was thin and short and, frankly, did not enjoy watching or participating in sports—a fact that came as a major disappointment to his stepfather, who had been an amateur boxer. "I can't stand seeing other people excel at something I can't do," Murphy later told Richard Corliss in "The Good Little Bad Little Boy" for *Time*.

By the time he enrolled at Roosevelt Junior-Senior High School, Eddie had made up his mind about his future: He planned to go into standup comedy. "I used to come home with report cards when I was 15 with zeroes on them and 50s and 60s," he recalled to Frank Sanello. "My mother would say, 'What's wrong with you?' And I would say, 'I'm going to be famous, Ma.'"

As a young boy, Eddie developed a true talent for mimicry. He found he could imitate the voices of such cartoon characters as Dudley Do-Right, Bullwinkle, and Sylvester the Cat. He spent hours watching old movies on TV as well, and was able to perform imitations of such comic actors as Stan Laurel, Oliver Hardy, and Jerry Lewis. After watching TV, he would often lock himself in his room, where he practiced impersonating the characters from his favorite shows. Murphy later said to Sanello, "My mother says I never talked in my own voice—always cartoon characters. Dudley Do-Right, Bullwinkle. I used to do Sylvester the Cat ('Thuffferin' thucotash') all the time. I could always get my brother Charlie mad by doing Bela Lugosi. Get him in trouble. I was that kind of kid."

Eddie did not just do his act for family members; each day, he would gather his friends in his basement and perform for them—he perfected dead-on imitations of Bill Cosby as well as singers Elvis Presley, Lionel Ritchie, Al Green, and others. At school, he was regarded as the class clown. His natural talent helped him stand out among other students. In fact, his talent to make his classmates laugh surfaced in elementary school. Murphy said to Corliss, "One day in the third grade, Mr. Wunch came into the classroom and said whoever makes up the best story would win an Eskimo Pie. I cracked the kids up with a story about rice and Orientals. It was my first performance. And guess who won the pie?"

Haith recalls that Murphy was always quick with an insult, always making fun of other students—the way they talked, the way they dressed, the way they walked, whatever. At Roosevelt, trading insults was known as "ranking," and, well, nobody outranked Eddie. "I used to rank on the kids at school by saying things like 'your mama got a wooden leg with a kickstand,'" Murphy said in an interview with *Jet*. "I was the king of rank." If anybody else had leveled the insults, Haith said, it is likely that a fight would have broken out. Eddie, however, had a way of making everything seem so funny that no one took offense, and everyone found a way to laugh at Eddie's gags. "I remember Eddie telling me one day that he made up his mind to be a comic," Haith said. "He loved having the ability to make people laugh and it was an ability that not everyone had. It made him feel good and special and important to be able to make people laugh and somehow I understood exactly what he meant."

THE LITTLE CELEBRITY

Eddie made his first appearance on the stage at the age of 15, hosting a talent show at the Roosevelt Youth Center. He wore a loud green jacket and matching green tie. Between acts, he told jokes and performed impersonations—getting the most laughs for a routine mocking Elvis Presley. His first appearance on stage also marked the first time he would use profanity as part of his act. Many of the parents in the audience later complained about the emcee's reliance on foul language, but he shrugged off the criticism. His foul-mouthed humor had drawn big laughs. Standing on stage, listening to the audience roar in laughter, "I looked *soooo* good to those little girls. They'd squeal at my every move. Looking out at the audience, I knew that it was show biz for the rest of my life," Murphy recalled to Corliss in "The Good Little Bad Little Boy."

Back in school that fall, Eddie formed a rock band and entertained during assemblies. Backed by his band, he would sing, but mostly he told jokes. He recalled to Rensen in their *Playboy* interview:

> I was like a little celebrity. I had already been on local cable. . . . In high school, I used to give assemblies. I did a show for six grades over three days. My band played, and afterward, I did an hour of material about the school: impressions of the teachers, students, hall monitors; there were routines about smoking marijuana behind the school, and getting caught by the truant officer, and cutting class, and detention, and gym. By the third day, people were sitting in the aisles.

It did not take long for Eddie to take his act to the professional stage. While still in high school, he started performing his standup routine at nightclubs on Long Island, earning $25 or $50 a week. He soon became a regular at the White House Inn in Massapequa and the East Side Comedy Club in Huntington. For a brief time, he hooked up with a couple of white comics, Rob Bartlett and Bob Nelson. They called themselves the Identical Triplets, finding work as entertainers at private parties, small conventions, and business meetings. One time, the Identical Triplets were booked to perform their standup act at a meeting of teachers. They took the stage during the cocktail hour and soon found very few of the people in attendance were paying attention to the jokes. It was the type of gig that was common for young unknown comedians. At one point during the performance, Eddie became so frustrated that he took the microphone and warned the audience members not to ignore him because in a couple of years they would be catching his act on *The Tonight Show*.

Despite those types of bookings, Eddie remained relentless in his resolve to find work as a standup comic. He was constantly calling nightclub owners looking for gigs—not just on Long Island but in nearby places as well. "You really couldn't leave him alone," said his mother, as quoted by Dalton and Hirshey in "Eddie Murphy: The Prince of Comedy."

> He'd be on the phone all day, calling Connecticut, New York, New Jersey, trying to find work. I got our phone bill, and I was sitting at the table looking at the long-distance sheets, and I said, "Eddie, look at this. What am I going to do with you?" And he looked at me and said, I don't ever want to be middle class."

Of course, spending nights and weekends on comedy club stages did little to help him in the classroom. Sometimes, Eddie would perform in clubs until the early hours of the morning, then crawl into bed just as dawn was breaking. A short time later, Lynch would arrive home from work and rouse his sons out of bed. Barely able to drag himself out of bed, he often skipped school by calling friends whose parents both worked and asking to sleep in their rooms while no one was home.

By keeping those type of hours and skipping school regularly, it came as little surprise to Eddie when he flunked the tenth grade. Under pressure from his parents, he managed to keep up with his studies. He attended summer school to make up some courses, took others at night, and was able to graduate from high school, albeit a few months late. "I was articulate, with a strong vocabulary, but most of the courses bored me," Murphy said to Corliss. "I mean, $E=mc^2$? Who gives a damn? My focus was my comedy. You could usually find me in the lunchroom trying out my routines on the kids to perform them in clubs later that night." David Better, one of his high-school teachers, told Dalton and Hirshey: "With Eddie, it was like he was here, but his mind was elsewhere. You got the feeling he had things worked out for himself and he was just putting in time here until he could go do them." Indeed, in his high-school yearbook, Eddie made it clear what he intended to do with the rest of his life. Under his graduation picture, Murphy wrote, as quoted by Sanello in *Eddie Murphy: The Life and Times of a Comic on the Edge*, "All men are sculptors, constantly chipping away the unwanted parts of their lives, trying to create their idea of a masterpiece. Future plans: comedian."

BREAKING INTO COMEDY

After high school, Murphy enrolled at Nassau Community College on Long Island, mostly to satisfy his mother, but by now he had no more interest in schoolwork than he had had in high school. Again, nights and weekends found him performing his standup routines in Long Island comedy clubs. Murphy soon realized that his options were limited in the tiny Long Island clubs, where the pay was paltry. Indeed, the bigger paydays—and the potential to find fame—awaited him in New York City. So he started auditioning for Manhattan comedy club owners, but few of them found his comedy, particularly his earthy language, much to their taste.

His first stop was the Improv, New York's premier improvisational comedy club for up-and-coming talent. When club owner Silva Friedman heard Murphy's obscenity-laden routine, however, she turned him down flat. Still, Murphy attended many of the shows at the Improv to see what type of material was making people laugh. One time, he caught the act of a young African-American comedian, Keenan Ivory Wayans, who would go on to a career as a major TV and film star. After watching Wayans perform, Murphy snuck backstage, found Wayans, and said, as quoted by Sanello: "Hi, I'm Eddie Murphy. I thought I was the only funny black guy in New York. Now I see there are two." Wayans was not put off by Murphy's brashness; instead, he was impressed with Murphy's maturity and found himself bonding with the younger comic.

Murphy's next stop was the Comic Strip, another club specializing in improvisational comedy. He won the audition with the help of Nelson, his former Identical Triplets partner,

In this April 1985 photo, Eddie Murphy is seen impersonating fellow comedian Bill Cosby during his standup routine. Murphy's uncanny mimicry, impeccable timing, and delivery endeared him to live audiences even when he first began performing as a teenager.

who knew club owners Robert Wachs and Richard Tienken and urged them to give the young comic a tryout. Wachs found Murphy arrogant and not particularly funny: He felt the jokes were unoriginal. Yet he could see energy in Murphy's audition, so he agreed to give him a chance to appear before a Comic Strip audience. A few nights later, in an appearance at the Comic Strip, Murphy wowed the audience. Watching the reaction of the crowd, Wachs and Tienken recognized the star potential of the young comedian.

In addition to owning the Comic Strip, Wachs and Tienken also kept a stable of young comics under contract, managing their careers and finding them work in other clubs. Murphy accepted their offer of a management contract. Wachs and Tienken took the young comedian under their wings and found him bookings at comedy clubs along the East Coast. "Eddie Murphy's career became a passion to me," said Wachs, as quoted by Dalton and Hirshey in "Eddie Murphy: The Prince of Comedy." "I dropped almost everything in my life to do this. I developed tunnel vision when it came to Eddie Murphy. Nobody his age has created this much excitement since I don't know who. I knew what he was and what he was capable of."

Wayans caught Murphy's act in those early days. He said, as quoted by Sanello in *Eddie Murphy: The Life and Times of a Comic on the Edge*:

> Everybody talked about his presence. He had an amazing amount of confidence on stage. His stage presence was years beyond his material. At 14, 15, your material is limited in terms of what you've experienced, so it's juvenile. But Eddie had a command of stage and audience that people ten years senior could only wish for.

Not all veteran comics were impressed. The comedian Rodney Dangerfield was in the audience for a Murphy performance at a club in Florida. After the show, Murphy ran into Dangerfield in the men's room. Murphy was in awe of the older comic, who had been performing standup since the 1950s and was, by then, a major TV and film star as well. Murphy asked Dangerfield what he thought of his act. Dangerfield told him that he enjoyed the jokes but urged him to cut out the foul language.

Murphy elected to ignore Dangerfield's counsel. "I'm not taking his . . . advice," Murphy decided, as quoted by Sanello. "How old was he when he got famous? In his 50s?"

Still just 19 years old, Eddie Murphy had no plans to wait that long.

3

The *SNL* Years

A few minutes before 1 A.M. on a Sunday in 1981, the producers of *Saturday Night Live* realized they had a major problem: The night's broadcast was falling more than four minutes short of material. NBC's weekly live comedy show, known familiarly as *SNL*, was supposed to run 90 minutes, but the producers had miscalculated the length of the sketches. It was becoming obvious that this episode of *SNL* was in danger of ending with what is known in the broadcast industry as dead air. Later, the producers discovered the reason for their miscalculation—a few seconds of "laugh time" by the audience had been calculated into each of the show's segments, but this episode's material was so flat that few people in the studio audience were laughing. Therefore, each sketch was ending a few seconds early, and as the conclusion of the show approached that time had accumulated into four minutes.

As the clock ticked toward the end of the show, *SNL*'s head producer, Jean Doumanian, summoned Eddie Murphy and told him to perform four minutes of his standup act. Murphy had been with the show for the entire season but until then had never had a substantial role.

Of course, as anyone who had seen Murphy perform standup comedy in a nightclub knew, his jokes included an abundance of profanity. He assured Doumanian that he would clean up his jokes for TV and, at 12:56 A.M., Murphy stood in front of the cameras and performed four minutes of his act for a national TV audience.

Watching at home, Murphy's comanager Richard Tienken found himself awed as the young comic got more laughs in four minutes than the rest of the *SNL* cast had been able to muster in the preceding 86 minutes. Tienken could tell that most of his client's jokes were ad-libbed. "That is when we knew we really had something," Tienken said to Joseph Dalton and David Hirshey in "Eddie Murphy: The Prince of Comedy."

DISASTROUS SEASON

Eddie Murphy had come to this moment because *SNL* was suffering through what viewers and critics saw as its worst season ever. During its first five years on the air, beginning in 1975, *Saturday Night Live* had proved to be one of the funniest shows on TV, providing audiences with cutting-edge humor performed by some of the most talented young comedians in America. Comedians such as Chevy Chase, Bill Murray, John Belushi, and Dan Aykroyd became stars virtually overnight; all would go on to careers in the movies. When the contracts for Belushi, Aykroyd, and the other original cast members expired, they were free to pursue other projects. At the NBC television network, *SNL* premiered in the fall of 1980 with a completely new cast of stars.

That season would prove to be a disaster. The new cast members, featuring Charles Rocket, Denny Dillon, and Gail

Matthius, hardly measured up to the talents of Belushi, Aykroyd, Murray, and the others. Audiences tuned out.

Murphy was hired for the show after another black comic, Robert Townsend, won the role but told the producers he could not make up his mind about joining the cast. (Townsend's hesitancy to join the *SNL* cast turned out to be wise—while Rocket, Dillon, Matthius, and the other 1980 cast members soon found their careers drifting into oblivion, no doubt thanks to their connection with their disastrous year on *SNL*, Townsend went on to enjoy a successful career as a film actor.)

As for Murphy, he won the audition after spending several days badgering *SNL*'s talent coordinator, Neil Levy, for a try-out. Levy recalled to Tom Shales and James Andrew Miller for *Live From New York: An Uncensored History of Saturday Night Live*:

> I brought him in for an audition, and he did a four-minute piece of him acting out three characters up in Harlem— one guy was instigating the others to fight—and it was absolutely brilliant. The timing, the characterizations— talent was just shooting out of him. And I went, "Wow," and I took him to see Jean [Doumanian] and I said, "Jean, you've got to see this." He did his audition for Jean, and she sent him out of the room and she said to me, "Well, he's

DID YOU KNOW?

It should not have come as a shock to anyone that the 1980–1981 version of *Saturday Night Live* flopped with viewers—it was the casting. In addition to failing to fully use the talents of Eddie Murphy, the producers passed over such budding talent as Jim Carrey, who has gone on to be a major Hollywood star, with leading roles in such films as *The Mask* (1994), *Dumb and Dumber* (1994), *The Truman Show* (1998), *Man on the Moon* (1998), *Bruce Almighty* (2003), and *Lemony Snicket's A Series of Unfortunate Events* (2004).

good but I like Robert Townsend better." And I went nuts, you know. I threatened to quit. At that point, there were so many mistakes, I was actually heartbroken, because I'd been on the original show, and it went beyond mistakes for me. It was like there was a spirit that I knew existed in that show and she had no idea what that was, and she was missing it. She would choose Robert Townsend over Eddie Murphy—not that Robert Townsend isn't great, a good actor, but the difference in terms of what was right for the show was so obvious.

After Townsend passed on *SNL*, Doumanian relented and hired Murphy for the cast—but not as one of the stars, who were known as the "Not Ready for Prime-Time Players." Rather, Murphy was credited as a "featured player," a role the young comic found irritating but—still an unknown at the age of 19—not one he was willing to turn down. He said, as quoted by Frank Sanello, "They told me I was a featured player—that meant an extra, really. I should have been happy even to be part of the show, but I looked at the rest of the cast—I'm not saying I was better—I just knew I was as good as any of the regulars."

TIME TO CLEAN HOUSE

After joining the cast, Murphy could not help but feel as though his role on the show included an element of stereotyping. Whenever the writers needed to insert a black character in a sketch, Murphy was given that part to play—often as a street hustler or a kid carrying a boom box. During the Belushi-Aykroyd-Murray years, that role was played by Garrett Morris, who was a very funny comedian as well as a good soldier. During his years on *SNL*, he never voiced a complaint about the nature of the roles he was given to play. Murphy had no intentions of turning into another Garrett Morris. He did complain, but his complaints often fell on deaf ears.

Even though Doumanian was not ready to showcase Murphy, the other cast members as well as the writers did recognize his talent and begged Doumanian to use him more. One of Murphy's closest allies on the show was a very funny comedian, Joe Piscopo, who was emerging as the star of that troubled season. It seemed Piscopo was the only Not Ready for Prime-Time Player capable of getting a laugh. Murphy and Piscopo grew close, often testing new material on each other.

Meanwhile, others connected with the show were able to see Murphy's potential as well. "He made me laugh the first day I met him," said *SNL* writer James Downey in Shales and Miller's book. "And he was just so clearly the funniest person on the floor. I remember saying to Jean Doumanian, 'You've got to use this kid Eddie Murphy, you've got to put him on.' And I remember her going, 'He's not ready.' "

As the dismal 1980–1981 TV season drew to a close, NBC executives took a hard look at *SNL*. With their longtime hit now a ratings bust, it did not take long for them to clean house. Doumanian was fired, as were many of the writers and most cast members. In fact, the only two cast members asked to return for the next season were Piscopo and Murphy.

SNL'S NEW STAR

When the new version of *SNL* debuted in the fall of 1981, Murphy was no longer a "featured" performer. He was now a full-fledged member of the Not Ready for Prime-Time Players. He would soon surface as one of the major stars of *SNL*. Recognizing his talent, the new writers fed Murphy plenty of funny material. Barry Blaustein, who wrote for the show in the 1981–1982 season, recalled to Shales and Miller the first sketch written specifically for Murphy:

> My dad was always calling me with ideas for sketches, and they were always terrible, but this was one time he came up with an idea that was decent. He'd read this article about a

high school basketball team in Cleveland, where the court ruled that there had to be at least one white player on the team. We wrote something for Eddie based on that, showed it to him, and worked with him on it. It was his first piece. And you could tell the first minute he was on the air that whatever "it" is, he had it. He completely connected with the audience. He just jumped off the screen.

Murphy worked closely with the writers, helping them create sketches to fit a group of characters he introduced on the show. All would prove to be fan favorites. Among them were:

Buckwheat. Fans of the old Our Gang (also known as Little Rascals) movie shorts from the 1930s knew the character very well. He was a young black boy, played by actor William Thomas, with rags for clothes and hair that seemed to defy gravity. Audiences had to listen carefully to hear Buckwheat's dialogue because he was barely understandable. Murphy, wearing an outrageous wig and beat-up overalls similar to those worn by Thomas in the films, emphasized Buckwheat's enunciation issues, vacant stare, and airheaded view of the world. When Murphy-as-Buckwheat sang the Lionel Richie hit "Three Times a Lady," the lyrics came out "Unce, Tice, Fee Times a Mady," according to Walter Leavy in his *Ebony* article, "Eddie Murphy: Will Movie Hit Create Problems for Controversial Comic?"

Mr. Robinson. The character was a spoof of Fred Rogers, the amiable host of the popular children's TV show *Mister Rogers' Neighborhood.* Wearing a sweater modeled after the one worn by Rogers, and speaking in an emotionless monotone similar to what Rogers' viewers had come to expect, Murphy hosted his own show—*Mr. Robinson's Neighborhood.* Only in this neighborhood, Mr. Robinson did not talk about the value of sharing or paying attention in school; rather, he was known to dispense such sage advice as how to beat the landlord out of the month's rent. Leavy recalled one Mr. Robinson sketch in

Here, Eddie Murphy plays Buckwheat, a character from the Our Gang short films of the 1930s and 1940s, in a sketch for *Saturday Night Live*. Murphy's embellished portrayal of the grown-up Buckwheat had the child actor retaining his wild hair and incomprehensible speech into adulthood.

Ebony: "Here's my landlord with an eviction notice," Murphy-as-Robinson said as he smiled broadly at the camera. "Can you say 'scrumbucket' boys and girls?"

Gumby. TV fans dating back to the 1950s knew Gumby as a lovable animated character who starred in all manner of adventures, usually assisted by his friend, an orange pony named Pokey. In Murphy's version, Gumby was a sarcastic, ill-humored, bitter, cigar-chomping, talentless standup comic. To assist Murphy in the Gumby sketches, Piscopo played Pokey as a whining, whimpering sidekick.

Little Richard Simmons. The character was a cross between rock 'n' roll pioneer Little Richard and exercise guru Richard Simmons. Murphy emphasized the effeminate nature of their personalities. In the sketches featuring Little Richard Simmons, he wore lip gloss, a wig of slicked-down straight black hair, and

Who Was Gumby?

TV viewers first saw the character Gumby in 1956 when he was featured in an episode of the children's show *Howdy Doody*. The tiny green character was composed of clay. His adventures with his sidekick, a pony named Pokey, would entertain children into the 1980s.

Gumby's creator, Art Clokey, used a process known as stop-motion animation to bring him to life. In stop-motion animation, the clay models are set up in front of the camera. To show motion, the animators move each figure slightly, then shoot one frame of film. Twenty-four frames are shot each second. Therefore, to shoot a brief film that may last just a few minutes, thousands of character manipulations must be made. The stop-motion process dates back a century. In the 1933 film classic *King Kong*, the filmmakers used the stop-motion process for several scenes to bring the giant ape and other monsters to life. Although the finished film shows the giant ape terrorizing New York City, in reality the filmmakers used an 18-inch model to shoot the scenes.

Under Clokey's direction, Gumby terrorized no cities. He was friendly, well meaning, and heroic. "The essence of Gumby is that he makes children feel safe," said Clokey, who died in 2010 at the age of 88. "He's their greatest pal."*

One would not come away with that idea after watching Eddie Murphy's impersonation of Gumby. Wearing a green foam costume and chewing an unlit cigar, Murphy's Gumby was foulmouthed and ill-tempered. "I'm Gumby, dammit!"** Murphy-as-Gumby would often declare.

For his part, Clokey could see the humor in Murphy's version of the little clay character: "Gumby can laugh at himself."***

* Mike Antonucci, "The Shape-Shifting World of Gumby," *Buffalo News*, December 28, 1997, p. E4.
** "Gumby Stumbles Back to Life," (Toronto) *Globe & Mail*, June 26, 1985, p. B12.
*** Associated Press, "Art Clokey, Gumby Creator, 88," *Philadelphia Inquirer*, January 10, 2010, p. B11.

Here, Eddie Murphy plays Mister Robinson, the ex-con who teaches children about the world while trying to avoid his landlord and the police, in a parody of the long-running PBS children's program, *Mister Rogers' Neighborhood.*

a pencil-thin moustache, while dressed in a skintight workout outfit. Murphy played the character with a lisp and placed him in situations in which he could poke fun at both homosexuals and out-of-shape people. During one episode, Murphy-as-Little Richard Simmons led an exercise class while singing his version of Little Richard's hit, "Good Golly Miss Molly":

Good golly, Miss Molly!
Looks like a hog.
Good golly, Miss Molly!
Looks like a hog.

Eddie Murphy performs on *Saturday Night Live* at Christmastime as Gumby, the popular clay stop-motion character that appeared on children's television for many years.

Oooohhh!
Well, you better start a-running
because it's much too late to jog
From the early, early morning
to the early, early night
You're just a fat disgusting blob of cellulite.
Good golly, Miss Molly!
Looks like a hog.
Oooohhh!
Well, you better start a-running
because it's much too late to jog.

Velvet Jones. This character was an entrepreneurial pimp trying to sell a "how to" book titled *I Wanna Be A Ho* on a late-night infomercial. "Are you an unemployed female?" Murphy-as-Jones asked his TV viewers, while smiling earnestly at the camera. "I can teach you to be a high-payin' ho."

Tyrone Green. A prison poet who famously recited the poem "Kill My Landlord" (Tyrone had a habit of spelling the key word in the title "C-I-L-L"), Tyrone was asked to give a poetry reading before a post of the Veterans of Foreign Wars during one episode. "Kill de white people!" he declared in front of a startled audience of white World War II veterans, as described by Sanello.

Raheem Abdul Muhammad. This character was a humorless film critic whose reviews were provided under a segment titled "Angry Talk." On one occasion, Raheem scolded the members of the ultraconservative Moral Majority for attending pornographic movies. "The next time I see one of them in a movie line I'm gonna put the majority of my foot up his moral butt!" Murphy-as-Raheem declared. Raheem also promoted soul singer Isaac Hayes for an Academy Award for his role in the two-fisted action film *Truck Turner*, a black exploitation movie hardly given high marks by any legitimate film critic.

COMPLAINTS ABOUT MURPHY

At 30 Rockefeller Plaza in New York, the headquarters for *Saturday Night Live*, NBC executives heard plenty of complaints about Murphy's brand of humor. Each week, a different group seemed to lodge a protest. Gay rights organizations complained about his portrayal of Little Richard Simmons. Feminist groups complained about Velvet Jones. Civil rights groups took issue with Buckwheat, Mr. Robinson, and Tyrone Green, according to Leavy in his article "Eddie Murphy: Will Movie Hit Create Problems for Controversial Comic?" Indeed, Franklin Ajaye, another black comic, questioned whether

Murphy had any "social consciousness." *Ebony* wrote, "In spite of his enormous success, some critics and blacks still have serious problems with Murphy's comedic material, which is often described as 'vulgar' and 'insensitive.'"

Murphy shrugged off the criticism. "A lot of old comics like Franklin [Ajaye] are just frustrated and, maybe, jealous," Murphy told Leavy. "I do Buckwheat because I think it's funny, and the character is too absurd, abstract and ridiculous to be taken seriously." As for the NBC executives, they were always ready to back their star. Audiences had returned to *SNL*, and the characters Murphy created kept coming back for more laughs.

IN HIS OWN WORDS...

Whenever Little Richard Simmons made an appearance on *Saturday Night Live*, NBC network executives knew to expect protests filed by gay rights groups. After Murphy used a derogatory term for homosexuals while appearing on a cable TV special, a gay rights group that called itself the Eddie Murphy Disease Foundation took out advertisements in *Rolling Stone* and *Billboard* magazines denouncing Murphy, claiming that he contributed to stereotypes of gay people. Murphy's response? Gay people should learn how to laugh at themselves. He once said:

> This is what I have to say about homosexuals. I am not the first comic to do homosexual jokes. When I said I was afraid of homosexuals, all of it was a setup for [a] Mr. T joke. . . . I don't have anything against homosexuals, I'm not afraid of them. I know homosexuals. . . . I make fun of everybody, I poke fun at anything that I think is funny. It's comedy. It's not real.
>
> I don't think homosexuals get offended by this. [Gays] who have nothing to do but sit around . . . and feel like people are pointing fingers at them—people who are insecure got offended. The way I feel about it is . . . because the majority of the country is heterosexual, and they read that the homosexuals don't like Eddie Murphy and they think, "Hey, all right!" They're wasting their money. They blew it out of proportion. . . . Do all the ads you want to.*

* Christopher Connelly, "Eddie Murphy Leaves Home," *Rolling Stone*, April 12, 1984, p. 26.

Even when he was not masquerading as Buckwheat or Mr. Robinson, Murphy found plenty of ways to find humor in gender roles, religion, and race. One night on *SNL*, he held up dolls of white actress Brooke Shields and black action star Mr. T, mimicking a love scene between the two dolls. Sanello, in his book *Eddie Murphy: The Life and Times of a Comic on the Edge*, quoted from the young comedian's routine that night: "I know Brooke's mom is at home right now having a heart attack watching Brookie kiss this tremendous Negro on television." Then, imitating Mr. T's well-known growl, he said, "Ah love you, woman. Mmmmm." After the usual protest was lodged, Murphy responded to his critics, as quoted by Christopher Connelly in "Eddie Murphy Leaves Home" for *Rolling Stone*: "My comedy's good-time comedy; conversations and fooling around with my friends, stuff that just happened to me. That's why I poke fun at everybody, because I'm not a racist, I'm not a sexist; I'm just *out there*. I use racial slurs, but I don't hate anybody."

INSPIRING A NEW GENERATION

The talents of Murphy—as well as some of the other cast members of the era, including Joe Piscopo, Mary Gross, Tim Kazurinsky, Brad Hall, and Julia Louis-Dreyfus—would help propel *SNL* back to its preeminent place among American comedy shows. Moreover, the work by Murphy and the others would go on to inspire new generations of young comedians.

Sitting at home, watching on TV, future *SNL* cast member Chris Kattan marveled as the comedy unfolded through the talents of Murphy and the other *SNL* players. He recalled to Shales and Miller in *Live From New York: An Uncensored History of Saturday Night Live*:

> I really got into *Saturday Night Live* when Eddie Murphy came on. He was so relaxed and had so much control and power over the audience and everything that was going on.

If there were no laughs he was still powerful, so relaxed and comfortable. He didn't get nervous, he didn't act like, "Oh my God, this isn't working," and rush through the lines. One time, I don't know what sketch it was, he made some mistake and the audience laughed, and he went, "Shut up!" I was like, "Wow, that was great." It's so great if you can be that relaxed and confident.... By the time I got to high school, I wanted to be on *Saturday Night Live.*

4

A Comic Genius Emerges

The scene that helped Eddie Murphy steal *48 Hrs.* from Nick Nolte occurred in the country-and-western bar, where Reggie Hammond impersonates a cop and intimidates the locals. That scene occurs well into the movie, more than halfway through the script. In Murphy's second film, *Trading Places*, he grabbed his chance to steal the movie from his costar soon after the credits rolled to open the film.

The movie is set in Philadelphia, where the audience finds Murphy, playing con man Billy Ray Valentine, impersonating a double amputee. Crouched on a wheeled sled, his legs folded under him, Valentine is panhandling—asking passers-by for money. This is no ordinary begging, though. Murphy plays Valentine as nasty, sarcastic, and pushy. When a young woman walks by, Valentine suggests an intimate relationship. "Once you have a man with no legs, you never go back," he tells her, according to Frank Sanello's book.

Soon, a couple of police officers see the con for what it is and jerk Valentine off his sled. As his legs unfold under him, revealing that he is not an amputee, Valentine declares that he has been miraculously cured of his condition and thanks the police officers for giving him a new life. Not amused, the police officers arrest Valentine. "Murphy steals the show," declared Leavy in *Ebony*. "In *Trading Places*, Murphy delivers a performance which indicates that he can become one of the biggest and best on the silver screen." *Chicago Tribune* critic Gene Siskel agreed, "His potential is unlimited. He's special."

NATURE VS. NURTURE

Trading Places was released in 1983, less than a year after *48 Hrs.* hit the screen. Murphy began filming the movie soon after wrapping up his work on *48 Hrs.* and while he was still a member of the *Saturday Night Live* cast. Indeed, between his popularity on *SNL* and his rave reviews for his work in *48 Hrs.*, studio heads were rushing to offer Murphy more film projects.

For his second role, Murphy again agreed to share screen time with an established actor, this time Dan Aykroyd, who had also gotten his start on *SNL*. The film tells the story of two evil billionaires, Randolph and Mortimer Duke, who make a bet: Can they take a street hustler, dress him up in expensive clothes, and train him to run their business? What would happen to their Ivy League-educated and snobbish executive director when they strip him of all his money and kick him onto the streets? The concept for the film was based on the so-called "nature vs. nurture" debate that has intrigued sociologists for decades. Are people born with intelligence, grace, and other positive attributes, or can they be taught to be smart and charming? Is it all up to nature, or can people's personalities be nurtured? In *Trading Places*, audiences got a very humorous look at the issue—a film that the TV network Bravo has included on its list of the 100 funniest movies of all time.

Another early film hit for Eddie Murphy was *Trading Places*, a 1983 comedy directed by John Landis. Shown from left are Eddie Murphy, as Billy Ray Valentine; P. Jay Sidney, as the Heritage Club doorman; and Murphy's costar, Dan Aykroyd, as Louis Winthorpe III.

Aykroyd was cast as the unfortunate snob, Winthorpe. The cast also included some other big-name stars, including long-time Hollywood actors Ralph Bellamy and Don Ameche as the evil Duke brothers. Murphy's role required him to do no more acting than he had done in *48 Hrs.* Essentially, he was playing the same wisecracking character. There were plenty of funny scenes in *Trading Places*, but also some thought-provoking scenes as well. During the film, the Dukes expose themselves as racists. Mortimer Duke, played by Ameche, expresses doubt whether the brothers will ever be able to change Valentine's personality, and that he will always be a con artist and thief. "What do you expect," Mortimer tells his brother. "He's a *Nee-gro*. He's probably been stealing since the cradle." As the audience soon learns, though, the Dukes have concocted an elaborate and illegal plot to corner the American orange juice market, exposing themselves as far bigger thieves than Valentine. It is Valentine, with the aid of Winthorpe, who uncovers the plot and turns the tables on the Dukes. Critics and audiences loved Murphy's performance, which helped the film earn more than $90 million at the box office.

LAST SEASON ON *SNL*

Trading Places was released as Murphy appeared in his last season on *SNL*. He did not want to return for the 1983–1984 season, believing his career would be more lucrative in Hollywood, but the *SNL* producers agreed to pay him $300,000 to appear on just 10 shows, instead of a full season's worth. Even that handful of shows would prove to be a chore for Murphy. His heart was simply no longer in televised sketch comedy. After one appearance, in which he played Mr. Robinson, Murphy admitted that the sketch fell flat. "I stank tonight," he told *SNL* cast members after the show, as quoted by Sanello in *Eddie Murphy: The Life and Times of a Comic on the Edge.* "I didn't know my lines. I was reading the cue cards for everything. I'm just burned out. I won't shoot myself. I'll just be depressed."

Still, for his last show on *SNL*, broadcast on February 25, 1984, Murphy turned in some truly comic moments. The show was hosted by Edwin Newman, a longtime network news anchor. In the show's opening sketch, Newman finds himself in a barbershop seeking a haircut from a couple of effeminate hair stylists, Dion and Blaire, played by Murphy and Joe Piscopo. Later, Murphy impersonated soul singer James Brown as he was interviewed by Newman. The highlight of the show, however, occurred when Murphy provided a satirical look at civil rights leader Jesse Jackson.

In 1984, Jackson was running for president and sought to be the nominee of the Democratic Party. A short time before the show, Jackson gave an interview to a newspaper reporter in which he used the derogatory term "hymies" for Jews and referring to New York City as "Hymietown." It turned out to be a very embarrassing moment for Jackson, who had devoted his life to fighting prejudice.

Virtually the only person in America who could find humor in the remark was Murphy, who ended his *SNL* career by impersonating Jackson and singing a song titled "Hymietown," voicing the lyrics much in the style of soul singer Teddy Pendergrass. "Don't let me down . . . Hymietown," Murphy-as-Jackson crooned to *SNL*'s audience. Later, the TV critics applauded the performance, calling it among Murphy's best work on *SNL*. "I'm just glad it's over," Murphy said later. "It was fun, though. Gonna go home, man."

CUTTING-EDGE COMEDY ON CABLE

While his performances for *SNL* may have been occasionally half-hearted, no one ever doubted Murphy's gifts as a stand-up comedian. In fact, a standup routine he performed on one night in 1983 is given credit for helping launch cable TV as a viable alternative to broadcast TV entertainment.

When Murphy performed his standup routine at Constitution Hall in Washington, D.C., the performance was filmed for broadcast on the cable network HBO, then known as Home Box Office. At the time, the cable TV industry was in its infancy: HBO's programming consisted largely of movies and there was virtually no original entertainment found on the channel. On this night in 1983, though, HBO cameras were on hand to film Murphy's act. The comic was in top form, delivering one of the funniest shows of his career. Moreover, his standup act included all the profanities he could not use on *Saturday Night Live*. When the performance aired on HBO, it was telecast with no censorship or cuts. The program, known as *Eddie Murphy: Delirious*, became an enormous success. Comedian Chris Rock later remarked to Chris Lee of the *Los*

Angeles Times, "*Delirious* was a combination of two things: great material and a great performance. I had never seen anything like it."

Murphy took the stage that night in an outfit he had bought earlier in the day at a Washington shopping mall: a pair of tight red leather pants and matching jacket. He wore no shirt. Murphy's brother Charlie said the choice of outfit was very important for Eddie—he intended to dress as no other comic had dressed for a TV appearance. Charlie Murphy told Chris Lee:

> Back then, the red leather suit was revolutionary. Most comedians dressed like bums. They looked unassuming and dressed down. The last thing you wanted to do was be pompous—project a threat.
>
> He came out as a rock star. Not the traditionally dressed, suited Bill Cosby. Eddie was wearing thousand-dollar belts, diamond watches, open leather jackets with his chest out.

During the show, it seemed as though no one would escape Murphy's comic jabs. He poked fun at gay people, even making light of the then-emerging AIDS epidemic. He imitated pop stars Stevie Wonder, Elvis Presley, and Mick Jagger. He made fun of himself, reenacting an episode in which his mother hit him with her shoe. The cable network showed *Eddie Murphy: Delirious* over and over again, always drawing huge audiences. Standup comic Byron Allen said that HBO aired so many repeat performances of *Delirious* that fans were able to commit the gags and routines to memory. "They memorized it when they were young and know it backwards and forwards," Allen said to Chris Lee. "They remember where they were and who they were with when they were watching it. It's more than a comedy concert, it's an event in their lives."

In part because of Murphy's performance, audiences learned they could tune to cable TV for the cutting-edge comedy and entertainment that was often censored on the broadcast networks. Under rules established decades earlier by the Federal Communications Commission, network broadcasters are limited as to how and when they can show so-called "indecent" programming, because such programming is available on the public airwaves. Since subscribers purchase cable programming, cable networks such as HBO are not affected by those rules. Today, of course, there are hundreds of cable networks, and many air uncensored programming.

A COP IN BEVERLY HILLS

Back in Hollywood, with two huge hits to his credit, Murphy and his managers started searching for a role that would enable the comic to carry the whole movie. Soon, the script for *Beverly Hills Cop* came to their attention. The script had been written nearly a decade before; over the years, some of the biggest names in Hollywood had been attached to the project, including John Travolta, Mickey Rourke, and Sylvester Stallone.

The story is pure cops and robbers: A tough Detroit cop, Axel Foley, heads to snooty Beverly Hills, California, to solve the murder of a friend. After Foley arrives in Beverly Hills, cultures soon clash as the wisecracking and rule-breaking Foley teams up with a couple of by-the-book and uptight Beverly Hills detectives, Rosewood and Taggart. Soon, the trail leads the trio of unlikely allies to a major narcotics kingpin.

Again, Murphy would be playing the same jiving street-smart character he portrayed in *48 Hrs.* and *Trading Places*. Unlike his two previous screen ventures, however, this time the director, Martin Brest, decided to give Murphy free rein to change the script and ad-lib as the scenes unfolded. For example, in one scene, Foley trails two suspects into a strip joint and tells the other cops that the two men were carrying guns in their jackets. In the first take, Murphy spoke the line as scripted, according to Sanello in *Eddie Murphy: The Life and Times of a Comic on the Edge*: "I saw bulges in their jackets." Brest decided to film the scene again, but this time encouraged Murphy to ad-lib. For the re-take, Murphy made up some of the dialogue on his own: "I saw bulges in their jackets, and that's a bit bizarre, having bulges on the way *into* a place like that."

Unlike *48 Hrs.* and *Trading Places*, Murphy would not have to share screen time with established big-name costars—this time, the other actors would be supporting him. Indeed, a large success of *Beverly Hills Cop* can be attributed to the on-screen chemistry Murphy developed with the two Beverly Hills detectives—Billy Rosewood, played by Judge Reinhold, and John Taggart, played by John Ashton. During the film, Rosewood and Taggart spend a lot of time trying to understand Foley's bizarre ways, but they soon find themselves acknowledging that he is a good cop and reluctantly decide to follow his lead. "Never has anyone as young as Eddie Murphy achieved comparable authority to decide what is hip and what is square," said *New York* magazine film critic David Denby. "Murphy is borderline insufferable. He's younger and smarter and nicer than anyone in the movie. Still, you can't dislike him. He only wants other people to enjoy life as much as he does."

A LOT OF LAUGHS

Beverly Hills Cop also made a statement about race relations in the United States in the 1980s. As a young black man navigating the predominantly white world of Beverly Hills, Foley learned to use his race to intimidate the wealthy and snobbish white people he encountered. Perhaps out of fear, or perhaps out of a sense of guilt, many of the white characters seemed more than willing to bend over backward to accommodate Foley's demands.

Arriving in Beverly Hills and in need of a place to stay, Foley picks the swankiest and most expensive hotel on Wilshire Boulevard. He walks into the lobby dressed in a high-school

(continues on page 44)

One of Eddie Murphy's most identifiable roles is Axel Foley, a streetwise cop from Detroit who must go to California to investigate a case in *Beverly Hills Cop* (1984). This smash-hit film, directed by Martin Brest, spawned two sequels.

Buddy Movies in Black and White

Trading Places, *48 Hrs.*, and *Beverly Hills Cop* are so-called "buddy films," meaning their stories center on the relations forged between the main male characters. In *Trading Places*, the buddies are Valentine and Winthorpe. In *48 Hrs.*, the buddies are Jack Cates and Reggie Hammond. In *Beverly Hills Cop*, the buddies are Axel Foley, John Taggart, and Billy Rosewood.

Buddy movies, particularly those that are comedies, can be very successful—they give the actors a chance to develop chemistry with one another, which audiences find highly desirable. Indeed, cinematic comedy teams date back to the earliest days of Hollywood when such teams as Stan Laurel and Oliver Hardy, Bud Abbott and Lou Costello, and the Marx Brothers made many films and found millions of fans.

What sets *Trading Places* and Murphy's other buddy movies apart from most Hollywood buddy films, though, is the interracial nature of the friendships. Murphy's characters, Valentine, Hammond, and Foley, are black, while everyone else is white.

Certainly, Eddie Murphy is not the first black actor to star opposite a white actor. The 1958 drama *The Defiant Ones*, starring Tony Curtis and Sidney Poitier, broke a lot of ground in matching actors of different races in equal parts. The film told the story of two escaped convicts, portrayed by Curtis and Poitier, who are handcuffed together. At first bitter enemies, the two men gain respect for one another and eventually become allies in their run from the police. Nine years later, Poitier again made a drama, *In the Heat of the Night*, in which he played a big-city detective forced to team up with a bigoted Southern sheriff, played by Rod Steiger, to solve a murder. More recently, the films of Gene Wilder and Richard Pryor as well as Mel Gibson and Danny Glover have also featured buddies of two races.

Film experts believe the Murphy films as well as the other contemporary buddy movies show a new trend in Hollywood—that blacks are no longer cast strictly as sidekicks, and that members of the two races can be accepted as equals by audiences. "American cinema often reflects the social rumblings going on in society," said Warrington Hudlin, president of the New York-based Black Film Makers Foundation. "The buddy relationship can be an allegory for the relationship between blacks and whites in America."*

Hudlin is quick to add, though, that Hollywood filmmakers are also business people who know they can sell tickets to black and white audiences when they feature black and white stars in the lead roles. "The other side of this is the buddy film is a way to reach out to two kinds of consumers: black and white," he said. "It depends on how cynical you want to be."**

In the 1958 film, *The Defiant Ones*, directed by Stanley Kramer, two chain-gang prisoners played by *(from left)* Sidney Poitier and Tony Curtis must overcome their racial prejudices in order to secure their escape. The film won two Academy Awards, one for Best Cinematography, Black-and-White, and another for Best Writing, Story and Screenplay—Written Directly for the Screen.

* Michael E. Ross, "Black and White Buddies: How Sincere is the Harmony?" *New York Times*, June 14, 1987, p. 223.
** Ibid.

(continued from page 40)

phys-ed department sweatshirt, blue jeans, and sneakers. When told that the hotel is all booked up and no rooms are available, Foley loudly accuses the hotel manager of racism. To avoid a scene, the manager finds a vacant room for Foley. Denby wrote:

> Murphy has the black man's intimate knowledge of what whites will give up to avoid a scene; he's a master of embarrassment—he plugs right into it and makes it work for him. . . . [*Beverly Hills Cop*] is very shrewd about race. It understands the exchange of aggression and guilt, and it's witty about the awkward way whites who have been taught to respect blacks will speak and act when confronted by an actual black man.

Of course, there was a lot more to *Beverly Hills Cop* than its on-screen chemistry and messages about race. The film featured a memorable soundtrack with songs provided by Patti LaBelle, the Pointer Sisters, and other top recording stars of the era. One song from the film, "The Heat is On," performed by Glenn Frey of the rock band the Eagles, became a hit on American radio. Moreover, the movie was simply a lot of laughs—and not all of them were provided by Murphy. A young character actor named Bronson Pinchot appeared briefly as an oddball art gallery assistant named Serge who spoke with a heavy European accent that was barely intelligible. Serge stole every scene he was in, even those in which he traded gags with Foley. Following *Beverly Hills Cop*, Pinchot went on to enjoy a successful career on TV as costar of the comedy *Perfect Strangers*, in which he played the role of Balki, a character very similar to Serge.

Released in late 1984, reviews of *Beverly Hills Cop* were mixed. Some critics praised Murphy's performance, declaring him a true comic genius. "Murphy knows exactly what he's doing, and he wins at every turn," wrote *New York Times* film critic Janet Maslin. Others criticized Murphy for essentially playing the same role he played twice before. A critic in the entertainment newspaper *Variety* remarked, "*Beverly Hills Cop* is more cop show than comedy riot. Expectations that Eddie Murphy's street brand of rebelliousness would devastate staid and glittery Beverly Hills are not entirely met." There was no arguing with the box office, though. *Beverly Hills Cop* earned more than $300 million at the theaters, at the time ranking it as one of the top-10 grossing movies in American film history. Eddie Murphy would never be just middle class, as he once feared. He was now a superstar.

5

The Softer Side of Eddie Murphy

A few months before *Beverly Hills Cop* hit the theaters in 1984, Paramount Pictures released another film starring Eddie Murphy. Titled *Best Defense,* the movie disappeared quickly and, years later, represents something of a blotch on Murphy's film career. *New York Times* film critic Vincent Canby wrote of the film, "It really isn't easy to make a movie as mind-bendingly bad as *Best Defense.* It takes hard work, a very great deal of money and people so talented that it matters when they fail with such utter lack of distinction."

Indeed, *Best Defense* is probably best described as a case study in how not to make a movie. The film was originally written and produced as a vehicle for British actor Dudley Moore. It tells the story of a weapons designer who defies his boss's orders and makes changes to the plans for a new tank. After reviewing the movie, Paramount executives found the story so lame and unfunny that they elected to shoot new scenes. A part was written for Murphy, who was drafted to play the role of a tank commander on patrol during a future war. When confronted with enemy fire, Murphy's tank is momentarily in peril but saved because of the change made, years before, to the tank's design by Moore's character. Moore and Murphy never share the screen at the same time and, therefore, never have a chance to develop any chemistry. Is it any wonder that the movie was universally panned by the critics? As Canby wrote, "*Best Defense* doesn't even make sense as a movie."

Of course, when audiences got their first look at Axel Foley, they soon forgot the debacle of *Best Defense*. As for Murphy, he aimed not to make the same mistake he made when he agreed to perform in *Best Defense*. Following *Beverly Hills Cop*, Murphy resolved to be very selective in the roles he accepted. He wanted only to make movies with big budgets that would be guaranteed to showcase his talents and would earn huge receipts at the box office. He also sought to accept only roles that would be critically acclaimed; he wanted no more bad reviews on his resume. As Murphy would soon learn, though, he would often have trouble meeting the very high bar he set for his career.

A BAD TIME IN TIBET

Thanks to the success of *Beverly Hills Cop*, Murphy found himself one of the wealthiest young men in Hollywood: Paramount Pictures signed him to a contract that would pay him $25 million for his next six movies. Now commanding big money in Hollywood, he formed his own production company, Eddie Murphy Productions, to manage his projects. His decision to establish the company reflected his interest in taking more control over his movies so that he could exert more direction over the path of the films. He staffed his production company with Hollywood insiders who were supposed to be savvy enough to know a winning project when they saw one. After the release of *Beverly Hills Cop*, Murphy's production company spent months sifting through projects while buying the rights to many scripts. Finally, Murphy made the decision: His first film following *Beverly Hills Cop* would be *The Golden Child*, a fantasy-adventure story released in 1986.

Murphy had big ambitions for *The Golden Child*. He asked Francis Ford Coppola to direct the film. Coppola, one of the most esteemed directors in Hollywood, had directed *The Godfather* (1972) and *The Godfather, Part II* (1974), two classics of American cinema. When Coppola turned him down, Murphy decided to direct *The Golden Child* himself. This time, Paramount executives balked. Because Murphy had no experience in directing, the studio's management hardly relished the notion of turning a movie with a production budget of $40 million over to somebody who was a relative newcomer to the movie business. (At the time, Murphy was just 23 years old.) Eventually, veteran director Michael Ritchie was brought in to head the project.

In *Beverly Hills Cop*, Murphy plays a tough cop from Detroit who leaves his home turf to solve a mystery in the strange and distant land of Beverly Hills. In *The Golden Child*, Murphy plays a tough private detective from Los Angeles who leaves his home turf to solve a mystery in the strange and distant land of Tibet. In other words, it was basically the same story, but without the chemistry that Murphy was able to develop with the supporting players in *Beverly Hills Cop*, including Bronson Pinchot, Judge Reinhold, and John Ashton.

Murphy took the role of Axel Foley after Sylvester Stallone turned it down; in *The Golden Child*, he took the role of Chandler Jarrell after Mel Gibson turned it down. The studio hoped that Murphy's sheer talent would resuscitate the project and, to a degree, he was able to help the movie garner sales at the box office of nearly $80 million. By most standards, such huge box office receipts should have satisfied the studio bosses, but given the fact that *Beverly Hills Cop* had

One of the first box-office bombs of Eddie Murphy's film career was *The Golden Child*, a 1986 mystical comedy directed by Michael Ritchie, in which Murphy played a private detective whose destiny was to save a child in Tibet.

earned more than $300 million, the business generated by *The Golden Child* was disappointing.

The plot of *The Golden Child* centers on an evil sorcerer who kidnaps a child who just happens to hold the power to save the world. Murphy's character, Jarrell, is enlisted by a beautiful social worker, played by Charlotte Lewis, to travel to Tibet to rescue the child. Lewis's character, Kee Nang, confides to Jarrell that he is the "Chosen One" who has been selected for the mission. The film contained something of a supernatural element: At the end, an evil spirit—complete with wings and fangs—made an appearance. Most critics found the plot silly and the special effects well below the state of the art. Of course, since this was an Eddie Murphy movie, Jarrell's dialogue included a generous amount of profanity, street talk, jokes, and intimidating language—in other words, the script could have been written with Foley or Valentine as the main character. Of the film, *Orange Coast* magazine movie critic Marc Weinberg wrote, "Simply, this picture is so busy trying to do so many things that it forgets that it's supposed to add up to something. . . . The story's neither coherent nor engrossing; you just don't care about it."

As for Murphy, he had little fun making the movie—particularly the location shots he was forced to film in Tibet. On one occasion, the movie crew filmed Murphy actually riding a yak, trekking up a mountain in Tibet during a blinding snowstorm. Taking advantage of the storm, the film crew shot a few seconds of footage that was spliced into the movie's trailer, later shown in theaters before the movie's release. As the camera focuses on a freezing Murphy, he complains, as quoted by Frank Sanello in *Eddie Murphy: The Life and Times of a Comic on the Edge*, "If I'm the Chosen One, how come I'm freezing while you're sitting in a warm theater? Chosen One, my behind! Why couldn't someone choose me to go to the Bahamas?"

Given Murphy's lukewarm enthusiasm for riding a yak through a snowstorm, it should not have come as a shock when, after the film's release, he read mixed reviews of his acting. Most critics pointed out that Murphy was still simply playing himself on screen. Critics such as Roger Ebert in the *Chicago Sun-Times*, however, did not seem to mind. He wrote:

> A lot of the time, he seems to improvise his smart aleck one-liners—I haven't seen the script, so I can't say for sure. What's amazing is that his dialogue always seems to fit. A lot of standup comedians throw off the pacing in a movie by going for improv at the wrong moments. . . . Murphy usually seems to have the perfect reaction, even when he's shocked to catch a wise old seer picking his nose.

In the *Washington Post*, critic Paul Attanasio seemed to be growing weary of the act. He wrote:

> The entire movie is tailored to Murphy, sodden with a sense that his every remark is hilarious, that his every smoldering look will have ushers shuttling back and forth with salts of ammonia to revive the women expiring in the aisles. *The Golden Child* is edited to Murphy's sloppy improvisational rhythms, so we watch him stumbling with his lines, searching for laughs he never finds. And, along the lines of his standup routine, most of the humor consists of Murphy approaching various thugs, Tibetans and special-effects demons . . . and offering to "break" what the delicate would call "the buttocks."

BACK TO BEVERLY HILLS

If the critics thought they would see Murphy expanding his range in his next film, they were mistaken. In 1987, Paramount released *Beverly Hills Cop II*. The script brought Axel Foley back to Beverly Hills, where he was reunited with the same supporting players from the original. This time, the plot found Axel teaming up with Rosewood and Taggart to investigate the attempted murder of a Beverly Hills police captain; in the process, they break up a series of daring armed robberies staged to finance an international arms-smuggling operation.

The film went into preproduction soon after *The Golden Child* was released. As that film earned lower-than-expected receipts at the box office as well as mixed reviews from the critics, Murphy was determined that *Beverly Hills Cop II* would be a hit. Prior to filming, he ordered the script rewritten several times until he was satisfied that it would best showcase his talents. Trying to satisfy Murphy, writers proposed a plot that would send Axel Foley on a case to Paris, where he could intimidate and insult uptight French citizens. Another idea called for the plot to send Foley to London, where he could intimidate and insult uptight British citizens. One treatment placed the story in Hawaii. Murphy rejected all of those ideas.

In the end, Murphy and the writers agreed that what worked in *Beverly Hills Cop* would work just as well in *Beverly Hills Cop II*. Once again, the script called for Foley to interact with the rich and snooty denizens of Beverly Hills, where he could have a lot of fun intimidating them with his street-punk language and antics. Given that scenario, some critics wondered why Murphy bothered to make the movie at all. Weinberg wrote, "The film is so consciously similar to the original hit that it isn't so much a sequel as it is a remake. We gain no new insight into Foley or his peers, but rather simply proceed with mindless action. Even the adventure is nearly the same—instead of stopping a classy drug smuggler, now Foley's after a classy arms dealer."

Other critics, however, continued to find humor in Axel Foley. David Denby wrote in *New York*:

> Murphy seems utterly at home anywhere. He's the star, the gravy train, and everyone in the movie treats him as a king. . . . He doesn't look vacant and bored, as he did in

The Golden Child. His eyes are alive, and he's volatile and resourceful. He has some great moments snapping his fingers in the faces of thick-headed criminals—his hand movements dazzle. He's still funny.

Audiences agreed, and responded to *Beverly Hills Cop II* in droves, helping the film earn nearly $300 million and making it as successful as the original.

BREAKING THE AXEL FOLEY MOLD

Finally, in 1988, critics got what they were waiting for from Murphy. In *Coming to America,* Murphy played a much different character than his fans were used to seeing: Akeem Joffer, a wealthy prince from an African nation who arrives in America, incognito, seeking a wife. Akeem did not spew profanities. He was not a street-smart tough guy. Instead, the film showed Murphy's softer side as he played a sensitive and naïve young man.

Coming to America was something of a buddy movie—the film costarred Arsenio Hall, a comic who is one of Murphy's closest friends. Hall played Semmi, Akeem's sidekick who misses the luxuries of his privileged life back home. Moreover, *Coming to America* was a romantic comedy—never before had romance been at the center of a film starring Murphy.

Murphy acknowledged that *Coming to America* would break the mold of what had always worked for him, but he could sense that audiences were starting to grow tired of characters such as Axel Foley and Reggie Hammond. "I trust my impulses," he said to David Rensen in their *Playboy* interview. "Rather than go for the buck, my impulse, after I did *Beverly Hills Cop II,* was to do something completely different from the [movies] I'd been doing. *Golden Child, Beverly Hills Cop, Beverly Hills Cop II* were the same character—Axel Foley—three movies in a row. After a while, people get tired of watching." Still, there were elements of *Beverly Hills Cop* in the

In *Coming to America* (1988), directed by John Landis, Eddie Murphy played Prince Akeem, an African prince who comes to Queens, New York, to find a woman to marry. With him is costar Arsenio Hall, who played his friend and aide, Semmi. The movie was one of the first in which Murphy played multiple characters.

Coming to America script. Just as in the movies featuring the Foley character, Murphy, as Akeem, played a fish out of water, placed into situations where he could milk laughs out of trying to understand the strange ways of a strange new place.

In making *Coming to America*, Murphy had tried to expand his range, but critics found Murphy's acting wooden. He had simply failed to convince them that he could pull off a romantic role. Writing in *Time*, critic Richard Schickel said:

Coming to America seems to be more career move than movie. After the raucousness of *Beverly Hills Cop II* . . . the star apparently wants to assert his claim on the currently vacant title of America's Sweetheart. His aspirations must be bigger and badder than that. We want—may actually need—something more from this gifted man.

The Black Pack

In the 1950s and 1960s, singer and actor Frank Sinatra surrounded himself with a group of Hollywood stars who became known as The Rat Pack. These celebrities included singers Dean Martin and Sammy Davis Jr., actor Peter Lawford, and comedian Joey Bishop. Other big stars were admitted into The Rat Pack from time to time. Together, Sinatra and his friends made a number of popular movies, including the 1960 caper film *Ocean's Eleven*.

By the 1980s, Eddie Murphy found himself at the center of similar group of talented actors that Murphy dubbed "The Black Pack." Among them were comedian and director Keenan Ivory Wayans, whom Murphy met as a teenager while launching his standup career; actor and director Robert Townsend; standup comic Paul Mooney; and comedian Arsenio Hall. "We have a group of about 10 that I like to call the 'Black Pack,' " Murphy said. "We basically hang out together and bounce ideas off each other."*

As with The Rat Pack, members of The Black Pack often worked together. Hall costarred with Murphy in *Coming to America*, while Townsend directed *Raw*, a documentary film featuring Murphy performing his standup act. The script for *Raw* was written by Wayans and Murphy. Wayans also cowrote *Hollywood Shuffle*, a 1987 film starring Townsend.

Although Black Pack members often pooled their creative energy, Wayans said the group was not as organized or official as the media made it out to be. "It's funny, but the Black Pack never existed," insisted Wayans. "It was something Eddie said in jest. It just sounded good, but it was never like an organized pack. We just happened to be friends. Eddie made a play on words, on Rat Pack, in the same way those guys were friends. Everybody in our group went on to make their own place, which is great."**

* "Murphy to do Fences as Part of New Paramount Contract Worth Millions," *Jet*, September 14, 1987, p. 56.
** Frank Sanello, *Eddie Murphy: The Life and Times of a Comic on the Edge.* Secaucus, N.J.: Birch Lane Press, 1997, p. 145.

Coming to America was a box office success, earning more than $120 million in receipts, but the film would cause extensive legal troubles for Murphy and the movie producers. In the film's credits, Murphy is listed as originator of the story, but soon after the film's release, two veteran writers, Art Buchwald and Shelby Gregory, alleged that they had written a very similar screenplay and showed it to Murphy. The two writers filed a lawsuit against the studio, claiming Murphy stole their idea. In 1990, a judge agreed and ordered the studio to pay Buchwald and Gregory a percentage of the film's profits.

Murphy may have had trouble selling himself as a romantic leading man on screen, but off screen he met his future wife, model Nicole Mitchell. The couple met in 1988 at the NAACP Image Awards. They would soon move in together and marry in 1993. Their first child, Bria, was born in 1989; eventually, they would become the parents of four more children. As Murphy said in Walter Leavy's article "Hollywood's $2 Billion Man Talks About His Marriage, *Beverly Hills Cop III* and the Joys of Fatherhood," for *Ebony*:

> A couple of years ago, I would have thought I would be confined by marriage, but it has been just the opposite. I feel loose because when you're married, you don't have to worry about stuff like your hair being combed and everything being right. You can fall out of bed in your drawers, hair all messed up, and you're in love with each other so she can do the same. It's not like, "Oh, I have to look like Eddie Murphy when she sees me."

6

Scandals in Hollywood

With *Coming to America*, **Murphy** tried to establish himself as something more than a wisecracking tough guy. When he failed to pull off the transition, he resolved to try again. This time, Murphy decided to take complete creative control over a project—he would star in the film, write the screenplay, and take a hand in producing the film, meaning he would involve himself in the business end of the movie. The film, *Harlem Nights*, would also mark his debut as a director.

Murphy had been itching to direct for years. After Paramount refused to let him direct *The Golden Child*, he continued to search for a project in which he would have total creative control. In the meantime, Murphy was growing into a more powerful presence in Hollywood. After *Beverly Hills Cop II* and *Coming to America* scored huge wins at the box office, Murphy knew he was in a position to dictate terms to the Paramount studio bosses and, in this case, his terms would include an

Harlem Nights (1989) was the first film written and directed by Eddie Murphy. Although it failed to appeal to critics, it was successful at the box office, if only because it brought together three generations of black comedians. From left are Eddie Murphy as Quick; Richard Pryor as Sugar Ray; Della Reese as Vera; and Redd Foxx as Bennie Wilson.

assignment as director. "All my peers were directing," Murphy said, as quoted by Frank Sanello. "Keenan [Ivory Wayans], Robert Townsend. . . . I was like, 'I'm the big cat on the block; let me see what it's like to direct.' So I did it."

When many actors decide to go behind the cameras, they often start with small, independent projects that help them learn the nuances of directing. *Harlem Nights* was anything but a small, independent project. In addition to Murphy, the cast included his longtime mentor, Richard Pryor, as well as other big-name stars, including Redd Foxx, Danny Aiello, and Jasmine Guy. Paramount gave Murphy a $30 million budget for the film.

Richard Pryor

When Eddie Murphy was growing up in Roosevelt, Long Island, he idolized Richard Pryor. Certainly, other black comedians used their unhappy childhoods and ghetto backgrounds as fodder for their humor, but Pryor's comedy included a certain edge: Yes, he was funny, but he was also very angry.

Born in Peoria, Illinois, in 1940, Pryor was the son and grandson of prostitutes. He grew up in his grandmother's brothel. It was a difficult environment for a child, and Pryor would often escape by going to the movies. At the time, Peoria was segregated, meaning Pryor was forced to sit in the balcony in seats reserved for black patrons. While that early experience with racism left a deep mark on him, the films he saw would also influence his life. A big fan of westerns and other adventure stories, Pryor dreamed of a life in show business.

Expelled from school at the age of 14, Pryor worked a number of menial jobs and occasionally ran afoul of the law but managed to keep his sense of humor. He had been acting in amateur theater productions since the age of 12; while serving in the U.S. Army, he took the stage during base talent shows, performing standup comedy for the first time. After his discharge in 1960, Pryor toured the country as a professional standup comic. Over the next decade, he would find himself much in demand as a comedian, appearing in major nightclubs and on TV. He eventually appeared in more than 50 films, including several buddy movies with his good friend Gene Wilder.

Murphy and Pryor finally met in 1982—they ran into each other on an airplane flight—and immediately became close friends. Murphy often consulted Pryor for career advice, even asking him if it was the right time to leave *Saturday Night Live*. "[He's] been very kind and generous to me, offering all kinds of advice," Murphy said. "I've started calling him Yoda,"*—the learned Jedi master of the *Star Wars* movies. Although the two comics remained good friends until Pryor's death, they did not act together until Murphy produced and directed *Harlem Nights* in 1989.

Pryor struggled with drug addiction for a large portion of his life. In 1980, he burned himself severely while "freebasing" cocaine. To freebase, users smoke the cocaine, rather than snort the drug, in an attempt to ingest a purer form of it. During the incident, Pryor was burned over more than half of his body.

In 1986, Pryor was diagnosed with multiple sclerosis, a degenerative disease of the central nervous system. Over the next two decades, he performed occasionally but gradually lost use of his limbs as well as a degree of his mental prowess. He died in 2005.

* Richard Corliss, "The Good Little Bad Little Boy," *Time*, July 11, 1983, p. 86.

Murphy felt he was up to the task. He said he had no fears about directing other stars and felt sure they would respond to his vision. Foxx, then 67 years old, had spent a lifetime in comedy as a standup comic and TV and film actor. Foxx said he was delighted to take direction from somebody who was 40 years his junior. "He's on top of the world, and he's doing a hell of a job," Foxx told an interviewer during the filming, according to Sanello. "He sure knows how to handle people with sensitivity. He'll come over to your side and give private direction—he never embarrasses anyone."

TURMOIL ON THE SET

Released to the theaters in 1989, *Harlem Nights* tells the story of a father and adopted son, Sugar Ray and Quick, who run an illegal casino and nightclub in Harlem, New York in the 1930s. The two men find themselves in a gang war over gambling in Harlem—the plot is filled with violent murders. Murphy took the role of Quick and cast Pryor as Sugar Ray.

Despite an abundance of talent involved in the production, things got off to a rocky start. Soon after filming commenced, Murphy fired the lead actress, Michael Michele, saying that he decided Jasmine Guy would be better suited for the role. Murphy had known Michele since working with her in *Coming to America*, in which she had been cast in a minor role. Michele told a much different story, alleging that Murphy had sexually harassed her and that when she would not agree to sleep with him, he kicked her off the picture. "Everyone thinks I should allow this to happen because it's Eddie Murphy," Michele told reporters, according to Sanello in *Eddie Murphy: The Life and Times of a Comic on the Edge*. "But if keeping a job means lowering yourself to the casting couch, then we're in a bad place. And if having integrity, ethics, and morals means never being able to work in the entertainment industry, then maybe I did choose the wrong profession."

Murphy steadfastly denied the charge, insisting that he never sought sex from the actress. Meanwhile, he found himself facing other problems on the set. Evidently, Murphy's direction did not suit Pryor, who found the younger comic ignoring his advice. In the article "Eddie Murphy, Richard Pryor, Redd Foxx: Three Generations of Black Comedy" for *Ebony*, Pryor told Walter Leavy, "I said, 'Eddie, with this shot, take the camera. . . . ,' but he just sat there and looked at me like I was a lost puppy." Later, both men denied that there was friction between them.

With so much turmoil on the set, it should not have come as a surprise to Murphy when the critics judged the movie a disaster; many, in fact, named it to their "worst movies of the year" lists. Audiences found the plot confusing and the writing weak. Murphy's acting was panned and so was his direction. Roger Ebert lamented in the *Chicago Sun-Times*:

> The movie stars Richard Pryor as a Harlem speakeasy owner
> and Murphy as his adopted son, and plugs them into a plot
> involving the usual Mafia bosses, crooked cops and sexy

IN HIS OWN WORDS . . .

Although the critics skewered Eddie Murphy for his acting in *Harlem Nights* as well as his direction of the movie, Murphy insisted it is a good film:

> I'm happy about the movie and I'm proud of the way it turned out. It's not an action-packed kind of picture, and neither was *Coming to America*. But I wanted to get away from that because [the critics] pigeonhole you for doing the same [movies]. Hollywood and Paramount would love me to turn *Beverly Hills Cop* into the *Police Academy* series, every couple of months, until *Beverly Hills Cop X*.
>
> Americans are creatures of habit: We like to do the same [things] all the time. That's why TV shows are so popular here. People like the idea of meeting somebody every week on a certain day, at a certain time, while sitting in the living room.*

* David Rensen, "*Playboy* Interview: Eddie Murphy," *Playboy*, February 1990, p. 58.

dames. There is not an original idea in the movie from one end to the other. Or maybe, come to think of it, there is one: The movie is set in 1938, and has all the right cars and clothes for that era, but the dialogue is distractingly contemporary. Murphy and Pryor are famous for their liberal use of four-letter words in their comedy monologues, but did Harlem dandies in the 1930s speak like standup comedians in the 1980s? I don't think so. There was an elegance in those days, a certain public standard of speech and behavior, that a rich black nightclub owner would have observed; he would have acted and spoken like a gentleman.

Most critics believed that the star had simply stretched himself too thin, taking on a major production to make his directing debut. Vincent Canby wrote in the *New York Times*:

Don't even worry about the fact that Eddie Murphy's name appears five times in the on-screen credits. The movie, "a film by Eddie Murphy," is presented by Paramount Pictures "in association with Eddie Murphy Productions." Eddie Murphy is the executive producer. The film stars Eddie Murphy and it was written and directed by Eddie Murphy. Though *Harlem Nights* may be an ego trip, it is a generous one. The only problem is that it's seldom as funny as it should be.

Although the movie made back the studio's investment, it did not make much of a profit. Overall, for an actor who could usually be counted on to deliver $100 million or more in movie profits, *Harlem Nights* was considered a bust.

PLAYING MULTIPLE ROLES
After trying to expand his range as an actor in *Coming to America* and *Harlem Nights*, Murphy decided to return to familiar turf. For his next movie, he reprised his role as Reg-

gie Hammond for the sequel to *48 Hrs.*, titled *Another 48 Hrs.* (1990), and then took another turn as Axel Foley in *Beverly Hills Cop III* (1994). While no one could claim Murphy was diversifying his roles, it was hard to argue with the box office receipts: Both films were very successful. His other two films of this era—*The Distinguished Gentleman* (1992) and *Boomerang* (1992)—were unremarkable both in terms of critical reception and box office receipts.

He followed these films with a truly strange selection: *Vampire in Brooklyn,* a 1995 film that attempted to mix horror and comedy that is regarded as one of the worst films of his career. In the film, Murphy plays Maximilian, a vampire from a Caribbean island who has made his way to Brooklyn, New York, in search of a bride. In addition to starring in the film, Murphy also served as the producer and a cowriter. To direct the movie, he enlisted Wes Craven, a Hollywood horror film director. Both men were eager to take on the project: Murphy explained that he always wanted to act in a horror movie, while Craven told reporters he always wanted to direct a comedy. Unfortunately, this mix of Murphy-style comedy and Craven-style horror failed to gel. Critics thoroughly panned the effort while audiences stayed away. A comment by critic Peter Stack of the *San Francisco Chronicle* pretty well summed up most viewers' and critics' feelings about *Vampire in Brooklyn*: "Murphy, as the vampire of the film's title, is the least interesting fixture in a story that gets muddled in its mix of horror and comedy genres: He is strangely cumbersome, which could be because of the hokey makeup and special effects surrounding him. *Vampire in Brooklyn* is neither funny nor frightening."

Despite the severe criticism of the film, there was a hint of something big to come in *Vampire in Brooklyn*—in addition to taking the lead role of the vampire Maximilian, Murphy also played two supporting roles, an alcoholic preacher named Pauley and a thug named Guido. Murphy has often experimented with the idea of playing multiple roles in his films. In

Coming to America, for example, Murphy can be seen, under heavy makeup, playing three minor characters.

Murphy has always admired the work of British comedian Peter Sellers, who often took multiple roles in his movies. In the 1964 Cold War comedy *Dr. Strangelove*, Sellers plays three of the film's biggest roles: British air force officer Lionel Mandrake, President Merkin Muffley, and the title character, Dr. Strangelove. Soon, Murphy had a chance to emulate the great Sellers.

In 1996, Murphy starred in *The Nutty Professor*, a remake of the 1963 film of the same name that starred Jerry Lewis. The story is, essentially, an updated version of the classic 1888 Robert Louis Stevenson novel *The Strange Case of Dr. Jekyll and Mr. Hyde*, in which a kindly and mild-mannered scientist invents an elixir that exposes his dark side.

In Murphy's film, a brainy, overweight college professor named Sherman Klump invents a formula that turns him into a sexy lothario named Buddy Love. In Murphy's version, he outdid Lewis in the original (as well as Sellers in *Dr. Strangelove*) and virtually every other actor who has played multiple roles in a single film. In his film, Murphy took on seven roles, including various members of the Klump family, both male and female, as well as Buddy Love and Lance Perkins, an exercise guru modeled after Richard Simmons, a celebrity who has been the butt of Murphy's humor since he created the character of Little Richard Simmons on *SNL*. The characters spanned decades in age—one of the characters played by Murphy was Sherman's feisty grandmother. Murphy's characters spanned the races as well—Lance Perkins is white with curly red hair.

Playing seven roles was not only intellectually demanding for Murphy but physically demanding as well. In the original film starring Lewis, the comedian played the professor as basically a nerdy character. Other than wearing a wig and some phony teeth, Lewis relied little on makeup to bring the char-

In *The Nutty Professor* (1996), directed by Tom Shadyac, Eddie Murphy expanded on the multiple role-playing he did in *Coming to America* by portraying almost every member of a single family. From left are Eddie Murphy as Ernie Klump and Eddie Murphy as Professor Sherman Klump.

acter to life (In the 1963 version, the character's name is Julius Kelp.) In Murphy's case, he chose to play Sherman Klump as a morbidly obese individual, in part to show the prejudice that overweight people often find themselves facing. In one scene, as Sherman bends over, another character shouts out, according to an article in *Jet*, "You got more crack than Harlem."

To transform himself into the 400-pound (181.4 kilograms) Klump, as well as the other members of Klump's equally obese family, Murphy sat in the makeup chair for as much as seven hours a day as makeup artists applied layers and layers of latex and padding. To head the makeup team, the producers enlisted Rick Baker, one of Hollywood's most renowned makeup artists. "For the Richard Simmons-type character, my makeup was from the ankles up," Murphy remarked in *Jet*. "They shaved my legs and painted me. I had to shave my armpits, and they taped body hair on me. I'm glad nobody can tell it's me after all that."

The Nutty Professor would turn out to be a critical and commercial success, earning some $200 million at the box office, despite the fact that Murphy was not playing the kind of swaggering tough guy he usually played. Sherman Klump is modest, polite, and, of course, nerdy. Critics congratulated Murphy on finally distancing himself from the character mold of Axel Foley, Reggie Hammond, and Billy Ray Valentine. "Murphy . . . is a comic actor of astonishing range," wrote Richard Schickel in *Time*. "He is able to invest his Professor Klump with an endearing dignity, give his lounge lizard alter ego, Buddy Love, an alligator's bite and then go on from there to play Klump's grandma. Also his mother, father and brother."

INCIDENT ON SANTA MONICA BOULEVARD

Professionally, Murphy had scored a triumph. His personal life was also blossoming—now married to Nicole, the couple had started a family. (They would eventually have five children together; Murphy has three additional children from other relationships.) In the early morning hours of May 2, 1997, however, Murphy found himself involved in an incident that made international headlines. Driving down Santa Monica Boulevard in Hollywood, Murphy stopped his car to pick up a woman. Behind Murphy's car, two Los Angeles police officers saw the woman get into Murphy's car and suspected that the driver had just picked up a prostitute. The police followed Murphy's car for about two miles (3.2 kilometers), then stopped the vehicle. They found that no crime had occurred, but the woman whom Murphy had picked up turned out to be wanted by police on a prostitution charge. She was identified as Atisone Seiuli and arrested. Murphy was not detained.

It turned out, though, that Seiuli was not a woman, but a man dressed as a woman—a transvestite. When the press learned of the incident, it became a huge story: Eddie Murphy, a major American film star, had been stopped by police in the company of a transvestite prostitute. Moreover, much to Murphy's embarrassment, it turned out that a freelance photographer had been driving down the street at the same time, saw the incident, and was able to capture several minutes on videotape. That night, the tape played on the tabloid TV shows.

Over the next several days, Murphy gave his account of the incident: With his wife and children out of town, Murphy had been unable to sleep. So he drove around town and, while stopped at a red light, saw what he believed to be a young woman standing by herself. Murphy said he could tell the woman was a prostitute and decided to strike up a conversation with her. Over the years, the actor said, he had often stopped to talk with prostitutes, derelicts, homeless people, and others, sometimes giving them money out of a sense of sympathy over their plights.

Murphy said he told the woman she was courting danger and that she should go home. According to Murphy, the woman asked him for a ride home and he agreed. Murphy said he was about to let the woman out of the car when the police pulled his vehicle over. Finally, Murphy said, he did not realize the woman was a transvestite until the story hit the news. "I thought Atisone was a girl," Murphy insisted, according to Kyle Smith and Lyndon Stambler in an article for *People*. "That's not even the issue. It wasn't like I was looking for someone. It was a person I assumed was a girl at the corner."

Tabloid reporters soon started finding holes in Murphy's story. For starters, when police stopped Murphy's car, he had already driven well past Seiuli's residence. Moreover, police said that the neighborhood where Murphy had picked up Seiuli was well known as an area where transvestite prostitutes plied their trades. Another reporter interviewed Seiuli's cousin, who said Murphy and Seiuli had already known each other before the incident. For his part, Murphy insisted that he was not gay nor was he cruising Santa Monica Boulevard that morning in search of sex. "It's embarrassing," he admitted, according to Smith and Stambler. "I'm not sitting around depressed going, 'Oh, people are going to think I'm not Eddie anymore, I'm not a man.' I know I'm a man, I'm a man."

7

Family Fun

It would hardly seem likely that a Hollywood star with a questionable-morals case surrounding him could change himself into an actor whose work would find appeal among young children—particularly an actor who had built his reputation on foul-mouthed comedy—but that is exactly the strange twist that Murphy's career would soon take.

In fact, the movie on which Murphy was working at the time of the incident on Santa Monica Boulevard was *Dr. Dolittle*, a 1998 remake of an enormously popular 1967 musical that tells the story of a physician who possesses the ability to talk to animals. Murphy's remake was no musical—in fact, the film resembled the 1967 version in name only. Murphy's version was set in a contemporary American city; the 1967 film was set in England and took Dr. Dolittle on an adventure to a mystical and exotic island.

One of Eddie Murphy's first forays into family-film comedy was *Doctor Dolittle*, a 1998 film directed by Betty Thomas in which Murphy played an animal doctor who has the ability to talk to animals.

Murphy said he had been working on retooling his image long before he accepted the role in *Dr. Dolittle*. No longer interested in playing tough-talking street hustlers, Murphy felt he finally broke away from that image with his work on *The Nutty Professor*. *Dr. Dolittle*, he believed, would add to his resume as an actor with wide-ranging talents.

When *Dr. Dolittle* was released to theaters in 1998, the media made sure audiences knew this was the first film featuring Murphy since his embarrassing moment in the company of a transvestite prostitute on Santa Monica Boulevard. Even so, film critics found the movie suitable entertainment for young viewers. "The adult in me might have liked the film to dig a little deeper into the human-animal connection, maybe get a little comic-philosophical," said *Houston Chronicle* film critic Jeff Millar, "but the 11-year-old boy in me says 'lame' to that and awaits the next . . . gag." As for movie fans, they did not seem bothered by the sordid incident in Murphy's recent past. They flocked to the film, giving *Dr. Dolittle* a robust box office take of more than $140 million.

THE FAMILY MAN

People who knew Murphy noticed that while working on *Dr. Dolittle*, his personality had grown more mellow. Known to be high strung and temperamental on movie sets, Murphy seemed more at ease. Friends attributed that to maturity—he was now 37 years old—as well as his growth as a father. On the set of *Dr. Dolittle*, Murphy enjoyed trading knock-knock jokes with his young costars Kyla Pratt and Raven-Symone, who played his daughters. "I don't think he misses his wild days at all," said his friend Keenan Ivory Wayans, as quoted by Samantha Miller, Michelle Caruso, Julie Jordan, Linda Shin, and Bob Meadows in "Dad to the Bone" for *People*. Indeed, now the father of young children, Murphy seemed to be taking his role as a maker of family-friendly movies very seriously.

Murphy also started spending more time away from Hollywood, preferring to live at Bubble Hill, the 22-room mansion in Englewood, New Jersey, he had purchased in 1986. At one time, Bubble Hill was considered "party central," but now Murphy made sure his children were growing up in a more appropriate environment. Joe Piscopo, Murphy's old friend from his *SNL* days, became a frequent visitor. "We sit on the front porch talking," Piscopo told a reporter about a visit to Bubble Hill. "We joked, 'What happened to us? We're dork dads now.'"

Dr. Dolittle was not the only family-oriented movie in which Murphy appeared in 1998. That year, the Walt Disney

The True Story of Dr. Dolittle

Eddie Murphy had a lot fun with his role as Dr. Dolittle, whom he played as a physician who learns to put his self interests aside to help animals. The character stemmed from a series of children's books that many fans were shocked to learn were at one time banned by American public libraries because of their racist language and ideas.

The 12 original Dr. Dolittle stories were written in the 1920s by British author Hugh Lofting. In the first book, *The Story of Dr. Dolittle*, the hero travels to Africa, where he is imprisoned by a tribal king. To win his release, Dr. Dolittle tricks Crown Prince Bumpo into freeing him from jail by promising to grant Bumpo's deepest wish—to be turned into a white man. In the story, Dab-Dab the Duck reminds Dr. Dolittle, "He'd never be anything but ugly, no matter what color he was made."*

The book also includes many derogatory terms to describe black people and portrays Bumpo and his mother, Queen Ermintrude, as actors in a minstrel show. The pictures were drawn by Lofting himself.

None of those details were included in the 1967 film version, which starred British actor Rex Harrison. When young people saw the movie, however, they flocked to public libraries to read the books on which the film is based. Kay Vandergrift, a professor of children's literature at Rutgers University in New Jersey, recalled: "When the Rex Harrison movie came out, all of a sudden there was a run on the libraries. No one had read them in a studio released the animated film *Mulan*, which tells the story of Fa Mulan, a young girl who disguises herself as a man and eventually leads an army in ancient China. For the film, Murphy provided the voice of Mushu, a dragon who is Mulan's sidekick and guardian. (Mushu has lost most of his dragon powers; to win them back, he must prove himself worthy by assisting Mulan.) Of Murphy's performance in the film, critic Ellen Futterman of the *St. Louis Post-Dispatch* wrote, "As Disney sidekicks go, Mushu is as memorable as they come. Murphy triumphs with the role, making Mushu lovable and irreverent as he tries to win back the respect of his ancestors by guiding Mulan."

while. All of a sudden, everybody read them and discovered the offensive passages. So many libraries banned them."**

By then, the Dr. Dolittle books were out of print—meaning no new copies were being published. In 1988, a publisher brought out the series again; this time, the stories were heavily edited so that the derogatory language was removed. The episode involving Prince Bumpo was also stricken from the new series.

Lofting died in 1947. His son, Christopher Lofting, maintained creative control over the books and insisted that the offensive material be removed. The younger Lofting, however, believed that his father should not be regarded as a racist, as such depictions of black people were common in literature that was produced nearly a century ago. Lofting said his father wrote the books to show that cruelty to animals is wrong—a theme that continues to be very important to many people today. Lofting had a chance to read the script to the Murphy version before the film was released. He said, "Some of the basic tenets of being kind to animals, some of those themes that were important to my father, survive in the script."***

* Jim Beckerman, "Ebony and Irony: Once Banned from Libraries as Racist, the Children's Classic *Dr. Dolittle* is Being Cast in a Whole New Light," *Bergen County Record*, June 24, 1998, p. Y-1.
** Ibid.
*** Ibid.

On May 8, 2004, Eddie Murphy and his wife, Nicole, appear with their family at the Los Angeles premiere of the animated fantasy motion picture *Shrek 2* held at Mann Village Theatre. In the four animated Shrek films thus far, Murphy has voiced the Donkey character.

SOME SURPRISE HITS

Not all of his movies were aimed at young audiences. Following his work on *Mulan*, Murphy agreed to star alongside comedian Steve Martin in a Hollywood spoof titled *Bowfinger*. The movie tells the story of a down-on-his-luck director, Bobby Bowfinger, who tries to persuade a big-name action film star, Kit Ramsey, to appear in a science fiction movie he plans to make. Ramsey, played by Murphy, refuses to star in the film, so Bowfinger, played by Martin, decides to make the movie anyway, secretly filming Ramsey then splicing the scenes featuring the star into the final print. To pull off the stunt, Bowfinger constantly sends actors—some dressed as alien invaders—to accost Ramsey on the street, where they speak their lines while

IN HIS OWN WORDS...

Following the incident on Santa Monica Boulevard, Eddie Murphy became somewhat reclusive, refusing to attend events to publicize his movies or to conduct interviews with news reporters. In one interview, Murphy expressed his distrust for the media:

You know why I get paranoid about journalists? The first thing I hear about myself every day is some new...rumor. Something comes out in the [tabloids] and seven people who work for me all have a copy. Every time I walk into another room, I hear, "Hey, did you see this?" I've developed this lowdown self-image because every day I hear something horrible about myself. It gets to be a drag, to say the least. . . .

I've heard everything about myself. The most ridiculous rumor was that I was [gay]. I don't know where that came from. . . . Maybe it's because I've made fun of homosexuals. The reasoning being, "He does a gay impression, so, well, he must be one." Then, I've also heard that I'm a notorious womanizer, which is sort of a contradiction in rumors. Another outlandish rumor is that I smoke crack, or that I do serious cocaine, or that I drink.*

* Bill Zehme, "The *Rolling Stone* Interview: Eddie Murphy," *Rolling Stone*, August 24, 1999, p. 52.

the befuddled Ramsey tries to figure out what is going on. The main gag of the film, though, is that Ramsey *actually believes* in flying saucers and fears that evil aliens from outer space are truly invading the planet.

In playing Kit Ramsey, Murphy was largely spoofing himself. He played Ramsey as a loud, arrogant, vain, profanity-spewing movie star. The movie also gave Murphy the chance to play multiple roles. In addition to the role of Ramsey, Murphy also plays a dimwitted actor named Jiff who finds his way into Bowfinger's cast. Well into the plot, Bowfinger discovers that Jiff is actually Kit's brother. "Murphy is . . . kinetic, a power source ready to erupt," *Los Angeles* magazine film critic James Greenberg wrote about Murphy's work on *Bowfinger*.

> He has so much physical energy, he can easily handle multiple roles, and here transforms himself into a second character, Jiff, a dim-witted cast member with a surprising connection to Kit Ramsey. In one of the film's hilarious set pieces, Bowfinger makes Jiff run across a busy freeway as traffic spins him around like a human top.

Bowfinger was a surprise hit in 1999, earning box office receipts of nearly $100 million. Another surprise hit that year was *Life*, in which Murphy and comedian Martin Lawrence play a couple of small-time crooks wrongly accused of murder. They are convicted and sentenced to prison for life—and spend the next 65 years trying to escape. As the story comes to a close, the two elderly inmates finally pull off their escape when they fake their own deaths.

Bowfinger and *Life* both proved that Murphy still had the ability to make people laugh, but another Murphy film from this period failed to connect with audiences. In the 1998 film *Holy Man*, Murphy plays G, a mystical figure clad in a white robe and exploited by TV executives who discover that he has the power to persuade viewers to buy products on a cable-television shopping network. *Boston Herald* film critic James Verniere wrote, "*Holy Man* should throw a bucket of ice water on Eddie Murphy's hot streak. It's one of those movies with a premise so flimsy you imagine cracks forming on the screen and the whole thing collapsing like a giant, plate-glass window."

If anybody doubted Murphy's ability to draw audiences to his films, however, they needed only check the long lines in front of the theaters for his next movie, a sequel to *The Nutty Professor*. This time, in *Nutty Professor II: The Klumps* (2000), Murphy played nine characters, including five members of the Klump family. *Variety* film critic Joe Leydon wrote:

> The interactions among the Murphy-Klump quintet are smooth, seamless and often downright astonishing, especially when one Eddie Murphy addresses another Eddie Murphy, then turns to embrace yet a third Eddie Murphy, who in turn says something to a fourth and a fifth. You're never entirely unaware that it's really the same actor beneath each accumulation of latex and foam-rubber prosthetics.

DADDY PLAYS A JACKASS

Three years after *Mulan*'s release, Murphy again provided the voice for an animated character, Donkey, in the 2001 film *Shrek*. The movie tells the story of a green, privacy-loving ogre, Shrek, who finds himself caught up in an adventure to save a beautiful princess. The voice of the title character was provided by comedian Mike Myers who, like Murphy, rose to fame on *Saturday Night Live*. Again, Murphy voiced the role of a sidekick, but his comic touch provided the film with a large amount of its charm. "One of the reasons I like doing animated films is that when they're done right, they're timeless, and my kids really get into them," Murphy said soon after *Shrek* was released. "I explained to them that daddy is playing a jackass in *Shrek* and they really got a kick out of it. They love hearing their father's voice come out of a cartoon."

In playing Donkey, Murphy was doing little more than voicing an animated version of Axel Foley or Reggie Hammond (without the foul language.) *New York* film critic Peter Rainer remarked, "Eddie Murphy's Donkey, who is so funny and so gloriously an emanation of the actor that, afterward, you might make the mistake of thinking Murphy was actually in the movie, braying at full comic throttle."

When actors provide the voices for animated characters, they read their lines in a sound studio. After the dialogue is recorded, the animators draw the characters so that the movements of their mouths match the words spoken by the actors (or, in the case of *Shrek*, which was a computer-animated film, the computer animates the images fashioned by artists.) Therefore, since the moving images are matched to the dialogue, voice actors are given opportunities to improvise—to go beyond the script.

Shrek's director, Andrew Adamson, was well aware of Murphy's improvisational abilities and encouraged the comedian to make up some of the dialogue. "Animation is a much more collaborative process than acting with my body and my face," said Murphy, according to the article "Murphy's a Riotous Shrek(kie)." "It's a trip to have the director ask for a small inflection in your voice, and then, when the scene is drawn, you see how that slight change brings out the emotion. Animation is different from live acting, where I concentrate on my body and face." Added Adamson, "The improv moments are gold. Eddie is wonderful the way he can take a line and completely make it his own. He might throw in a little wording, and all of a sudden it's like no one else could have delivered that line."

Shrek proved to be a blockbuster, earning nearly $500 million at the box office. Artistically, it was recognized as an achievement as well, winning the Academy Award for Best Animated Feature. The film would go on to spawn three sequels—*Shrek 2* (2004), *Shrek the Third* (2007), and *Shrek Forever After* (2010)—each featuring Murphy as Donkey.

THE WORST EDDIE MURPHY MOVIES EVER

Murphy immediately followed up *Shrek* with *Dr. Dolittle 2* (2001) and then another family-friendly feature, *Daddy Day Care* (2003), which told the story of an unemployed father, Charlie Hinton, who opens a day-care business in his home. (Since Hinton and the other unemployed fathers in the neighborhood have to stay home and watch their children anyway, they hit upon the idea of getting paid to watch other people's children.) The movie gave Murphy the chance to interact with assorted children and to milk laughs out of the various uncomfortable situations they force him into. At one point, the preschoolers under Charlie's watch ask him such questions as "Are dolphins fish?" and "Where do babies come from?" For "pet day" at the day-care center, in which all the kids bring in their pets for show-and-tell, most seem determined to explain the animals' bathroom habits. Andy Dougan, the film critic for the *Glasgow Evening Herald* in Scotland, found the movie's plot stiff and predictable but also found himself charmed by Murphy's performance. "There's no doubting Murphy's amiability in a vehicle like this," wrote Dougan. "Despite the blandness of the material his comic timing is unrivaled."

Although audiences seemed to love Murphy in his new family-friendly roles, the actor would take some missteps during this same period. He agreed to play in a buddy movie alongside actor Owen Wilson. The project was the film *I Spy*, based on a successful 1960s TV series of the same name about the adventures of a couple of secret agents. The original series starred actor Robert Culp and comic Bill Cosby, the latter at the dawn of his career, as the two spies. The series lasted four seasons on American TV, due largely to the on-screen chemistry Culp and Cosby were able to forge.

Critics found none of that chemistry between Wilson and Murphy. They agreed that Murphy was largely miscast—director Betty Thomas turned him into the straight man, meaning that Wilson had to make the gags work. In many of his films, the laid-back Wilson has been able to generate a lot of laughs, but this time the gags simply fell flat. Although the original TV series was staged as a drama, audiences appreciated the wry degree of humor generated by Culp and Cosby. None of that subtle comedy could be found in the film version. "The show . . . had a brain and a heart, and the heroes made for a genuinely interesting contrast," wrote Associated Press film critic David Germain. "Murphy and Wilson, though, are mismatched boobs, insufferable in their boorish bickering and unamusing incompetence." *I Spy* turned out to be a flop; it disappeared quickly from the theaters.

When it was released in 2002, *I Spy* may have gone down in history as the worst Eddie Murphy movie of all time, but the same year that flop was released, Murphy starred in an even bigger fiasco: *The Adventures of Pluto Nash.* The film, a combination of science fiction and comedy, tells a story about a nightclub owner on the moon battling gangsters. Given the technology available to moviemakers, the film was panned for its lack of convincing special effects as well as its shortage of laughs. Critics placed a large share of the blame on Murphy, whose acting was regarded as wooden. Reportedly costing $100 million to film, the movie earned box office receipts of just $7 million, a dismal record that quickly propelled the film onto the list of Hollywood's all-time flops.

DID YOU KNOW?

Eddie Murphy's interest in starring in a science fiction movie may have stemmed from his love for the 1960s TV series *Star Trek.* The original TV series ran for just three years on network TV but later spawned additional TV series as well as several movies, the most recent of which was released in 2009. In 1986, Murphy actually spoke with the producers of *Star Trek IV: The Voyage Home* about playing a role in the film, but the filmmakers eventually decided to produce the movie without him.

Writing in *Film Journal International*, critic Ethan Alter said:

> If *Pluto Nash* doesn't contain much in the way of comedy, what exactly does it feature? Well, there are a number of poorly choreographed laser battles, long, pointless conversations about why the moon is a better place to live than Earth, character actors ducking for cover . . . and a leaden romantic subplot. In short, it's everything you don't go to the movies for. Small wonder, then, that everyone stayed home.

8

Still Pushing Boundaries

After a career in films spanning more than three decades, the movie that would finally establish Eddie Murphy as a serious actor was *Dreamgirls*, which was released in 2006. Based loosely on the rise of Motown Records and the careers of the Supremes, the 1960s-era group of female singers, *Dreamgirls* was Murphy's first truly dramatic role.

He played James "Thunder" Early, a soul singer who turns to drugs when his career starts on a downward slide. For his work on the film, Murphy was nominated for an Oscar for best supporting actor, the first Academy Award nomination of his career. Although he did not win the Oscar, he did score a Golden Globe for his performance as Early; in Hollywood, the Golden Globes are considered a notch below the Oscars but still highly regarded. The film's director, Bill Condon, said he was shocked by the performance Murphy turned in on the set. Condon told Josh Rottenberg, Vanessa Juarez and Adam B.

Vary in "How Eddie Got His Groove Back": "I was so stunned every day by what Eddie was doing. I said to him, 'Why don't you do more of this kind of thing?' He said, 'Nobody ever asked me.'"

For Murphy, *Dreamgirls* arrived at the right moment in his career. Following *I Spy* and *The Adventures of Pluto Nash*, Murphy had starred in another dud, a 2003 comedy-horror film titled *The Haunted Mansion*. (The film, produced by the Disney studio, was based largely on an attraction at the Disneyland theme park.) In the meantime, he provided the voice for Donkey in *Shrek 2*, but he clearly was in search of a project that would test his acting skills. At the same time, Murphy's personal life was also going through a bit of turmoil—in 2005, Murphy and his wife, Nicole, decided to divorce.

When Murphy was approached about playing the role of Thunder Early, he was at first hesitant. It meant taking a supporting part rather than the starring role, which also meant the producers would not be willing to pay him big money. At this time, Murphy was commanding around $10 million per movie, but his fee for *Dreamgirls* is believed to have been a lot less.

CHANNELING JAMES BROWN

Murphy had been a fan of *Dreamgirls* since it premiered as a play on Broadway in 1981. After meeting with Condon and studio executives, Murphy agreed to reduce his fee and accept the role of Thunder Early. Murphy found himself joining a cast that included some of the biggest talent in Hollywood: Among the other stars of the film were Jamie Foxx, Beyoncé Knowles, and Jennifer Hudson.

During the filming, Murphy *became* Thunder Early, completely throwing himself into the part. The role of Early is believed to have been based on the life of soul singer James Brown. Known as the "Godfather of Soul," Brown recorded such hits as "Papa's Got a Brand New Bag," "I Got You (I Feel Good)," and "Living in America." Brown is regarded as a

Eddie Murphy's role as James "Thunder" Early in the 2006 film *Dreamgirls*, directed by Bill Condon, was directly inspired by music legend James Brown, also known as the Godfather of Soul. For his riveting dramatic performance, Murphy earned an Academy Award nomination.

pioneer of soul music, but he also battled drug addiction for much of his life and had several run-ins with the law, including an incident in which he brandished a shotgun and led police on a high-speed chase. That incident led to a 15-month jail term in 1990 and 1991. Brown died at the age of 73 in December 2006, just as *Dreamgirls* was released to theaters.

Eddie Murphy, Singer

In *Dreamgirls*, Eddie Murphy's voice can be heard contributing to five songs in the film. In fact, Murphy has been singing since high school and has even released three vocal CDs in his career, including *How Could It Be* in 1985, *So Happy* in 1989, and *Love's Alright* in 1993. His biggest hit was the single "Party All the Time," which climbed to second place on *Billboard* magazine's Hot 100 charts in 1985. The song was written and produced by the late recording star Rick James, who was Murphy's close friend.

The critics have never been kind to Murphy's musical efforts. Even though "Party All the Time" scored strong sales, in 2004 the magazine *Blender* selected it for eighth place on the publication's list of "50 Worst Songs Ever." Murphy has always shrugged off such criticism. "When I did my first record, I remember one of the things that a critic said was that I didn't really sing, that I did, like, impressions," he said. "So you can't really take my voice seriously, because I could be just doing an impression. I thought that was the weirdest thing I had ever heard."[*]

Despite the criticism, Murphy has never been hesitant about letting his fans hear him sing. In the movie *Shrek*, Murphy performs a cover of "I'm a Believer," the hit by the 1960s group the Monkees. In fact, of all the major players in *Shrek*, including Mike Myers and Cameron Diaz, Murphy is the only performer whose voice is heard on the movie's soundtrack album. "Quite frankly, he actually is a singer,"[**] insisted Marylata Jacob, the film's music supervisor.

As for *Dreamgirls*, the album received strong reviews from critics. Of the album, *Rolling Stone* said Murphy's performance of the song "Cadillac Car" is a "good facsimile of vintage Motown."[***]

[*] J.D. Considine, "Eddie Likes His Music Even if Others Don't," *Albany Times Union*, September 9, 1993, p. 2.
[**] "Eddie Murphy Breaks Out Into Song," (Toronto) *Globe and Mail*, March 9, 2001.
[***] Robert Christgau, "*Dreamgirls*: Music From the Motion Picture," *Rolling Stone*, December 12, 2006.

Of course, Murphy had been spoofing Brown since his days on *Saturday Night Live*, but for *Dreamgirls* audiences saw a far different interpretation of the soul singer by Murphy. Critics who saw *Dreamgirls* said they are convinced that Murphy found a way to become James Brown on screen. "Eddie Murphy plays James 'Thunder' Early in *Dreamgirls*, and no matter what anyone says, Murphy—at least for the first half of the movie—is playing a version of Brown," said Fox News critic Roger Friedman. "Indeed, when Murphy's Early bursts out into a funky rap on a live TV show later in the film, it's Brown he's channeling. No way around it."

Condon believes the breakup of Murphy's marriage had a lot to do with the intensity of his acting on the film. Murphy tapped into the inner turmoil he was feeling over the breakup with Nicole and transferred it to his performance. Condon told Rottenberg, Juarez, and Vary, "He would come into the recording sessions and just say, 'I can't go on. It's Christmas and my marriage is falling apart.' He clearly used some of the stuff he was going through."

Critics were impressed with his work. In the *Chicago Sun-Times*, film critic Richard Roeper wrote:

> Murphy deserves a best supporting actor nomination for his searing performance. Whether he's crooning a ballad or getting nasty with a sexually charged number onstage, rapid-fire quipping with the ladies and his bandmates or sinking into a drug-fueled funk, Murphy is riveting, not once winking at the camera or falling back on time-honored "Eddie-isms." It may be the best work he's ever done.

FODDER FOR THE TABLOIDS

Meanwhile, Hollywood insiders expressed shock at the announcement in 2005 that Murphy and his wife had decided to split. Murphy had long since ended his hard-partying ways and seemed to be enjoying family life. As for the couple, they released only a terse statement that said, as quoted by *Hello*: "The welfare of our children is our main concern and their best interest is our first priority."

Following his divorce from Nicole, Murphy has found that his relationships are often fodder for the tabloid press. At first, he maintained a relationship with Melanie Brown, formerly of the musical group the Spice Girls, then broke up with her after she disclosed her pregnancy. Murphy denied being the father and submitted to a DNA test, which determines, through a blood or tissue sample, whether the suspected father shares genetic traits with the child. The test did, in fact, determine that Murphy is the child's father. Later, a court ordered him to provide support for the child. (The baby is his eighth—five with Nicole, three with women from other relationships.)

In 2008, Murphy married film producer Tracey Edmonds in a ceremony in Bora Bora, a tropical island in the Pacific Ocean. That ceremony was considered unofficial; later, Murphy and Edmonds planned to exchange vows in the United States. Just a few weeks after the Bora Bora ceremony, however, the couple announced their intentions to split up and not go through with a legal marriage. Tabloid newspapers reported that Edmonds balked at signing a prenuptial agreement, which is a contract that would have stated, in the event of a divorce, that she would have been entitled to a preset amount of money. Under law in most states, divorcing spouses are entitled to half the assets of the family—unless they sign a prenuptial agreement limiting what they can receive as part of the divorce settlement. In Hollywood, prenuptial agreements are common among stars and their spouses.

THIN SCRIPTS

Since *Dreamgirls*, Murphy's career has seen its ups and downs. His first film after *Dreamgirls* was the comedy *Norbit*. As with *The Nutty Professor*, *Norbit* gave Murphy the opportunity to play multiple roles. *Norbit* is a comedy-romance in which

Murphy plays Norbit Rice, who fights to save the orphanage where he grew up. In the film, Murphy also plays the roles of Wong, the manager of the orphanage, and Rasputia, Norbit's evil and morbidly obese wife. As with *The Nutty Professor* movies, Rick Baker was enlisted to turn Murphy into Rasputia and Wong. "To play Rasputia, Mr. Murphy appears to have been encased in foam rubber," wrote *New York Times* film critic A.O. Scott. "It is when Rasputia goes out in a bikini (and, later, for a bikini wax) that the full extent of Mr. Baker's virtuosity becomes evident."

Scott and other critics mostly panned *Norbit*, finding the story and the jokes predictable. "Too many of the gags are lumbering and graceless, more fun to anticipate than to witness," Scott wrote. "What will happen when Rasputia goes down an amusement park water slide? She'll crash through a wall. What will she do when she's mad at Norbit? Throw him through a window." Despite harsh words from the critics, audiences embraced *Norbit*. The film was a smash hit, earning the studio some $160 million at the box office.

Murphy followed up *Norbit* by providing the voice of Donkey for the third installment in the Shrek series, *Shrek the Third*. Then Murphy made two flops—*Meet Dave* and *Imagine That*. In both films, Murphy returned to family-oriented entertainment. In *Meet Dave*, he takes on the unusual role of a spaceship that crash-lands on Earth. Inside the spaceship, "Dave's" movements are controlled by 100 tiny aliens. Critics couldn't find much humor in the story, but they gave credit to Murphy for trying to milk laughs out of the rather thin script. "This is a performer who, from his snapping, rubber-band mouth to his fancy-dancing toes, wrings comedy (and sometimes a little menace) from every twitch and tremble," wrote *New York Times* critic Manohla Dargis. "I could watch Mr. Murphy go herky-jerky for 90 minutes, but these bits of pure comedy have been predictably folded into the usual filler: a cute kid, a love interest, some plot."

Eddie Murphy laughs after being presented with his Golden Globe Award for Best Performance by an Actor in a Supporting Role in a Motion Picture for his role in *Dreamgirls* at the 64th Annual Golden Globes in Beverly Hills, California, on January 15, 2007.

In *Imagine That*, Murphy plays a harried executive who turns to his daughter's make-believe friends to help him solve his problems. As audience interest failed to materialize for the two films, *New York Times* film writer Brooks Barnes posed this question: "Why does Hollywood keep hiring this man?" Studio executive Jeffrey Katzenberg in the same article provided the answer: "He is explosive, given the right project, the right circumstances, the right director."

Certainly, Hollywood producers are convinced that Murphy still has box office appeal. Recently, *Entertainment Weekly* totaled up box office receipts for all of Murphy's movies and came to the rather astounding number of $3 billion. "I think his work speaks for itself," says Katzenberg, as quoted by Rottenberg, Juarez, and Vary. "I think it speaks very loudly for itself."

NEW PROJECTS ON THE HORIZON

Now well into middle age, Murphy has no intentions of slowing down. He has several film projects on the horizon and plans to continue making movies for years to come. In 2010, the fourth Shrek film, *Shrek Forever After*, was released with Murphy again providing the voice of Donkey. In 2011, two Murphy films are slated for release, including *A Thousand Words*. In the film, Murphy plays a fast-talking character named Jack who uses words as a weapon and has no qualms about lying when it suits him. Things are going well for Jack, but then he finds himself under the spell of a hex that leads him to believe he will die after he speaks 1,000 words. With such a threat hanging over his head, Jack is very careful about what he says.

For a comedian who started honing his language skills during his "ranking" days in high school, *A Thousand Words* represents a new test for Murphy's growth as an actor. In fact, in about half the movie he has no dialogue at all. Murphy considers the role a challenge—he must show emotion and make himself understood without speaking. Essentially, Murphy will be acting in the style of such silent-film comics as Charlie Chaplin and Buster Keaton, who were able to communicate with their audiences even though the film industry, at the time, lacked the technical ability to add sound to their movies. Kerry Washington, Murphy's costar in the film, said, according to "Eddie Murphy Channels Charlie Chaplin for Thousand Words," posted on the MTV Movies Blog:

> It becomes a Charlie Chaplin film for Eddie Murphy. It's hilarious. It's [also] this really, really lovely poignant film. It's just this fantastic story about a guy who learns to truly understand the importance of his words, and to say what he means. He doesn't speak his truth [at the beginning] so it's really about this guy having to learn how important his word is.

The other Murphy movie slated for release in 2011 is *Beverly Hills Cop IV*. Since the film will be released 17 years after Axel Foley made his last trip to Southern California, critics and filmgoers are eagerly awaiting how Murphy plans to portray an older, wiser, and mellower version of the wisecracking cop from Detroit.

Another future Murphy project is expected to be *Fantasy Island*, a film spoof of the 1970s-era TV show in which a mysterious white-suited stranger named Mr. Roarke, played by Mexican actor Ricardo Montalban, fulfilled people's fantasies by flying them to a remote island. Murphy plans to take multiple roles in the film version, including the role of Roarke. Murphy is also slated to star in a remake of the 1957 science fiction classic *The Incredible Shrinking Man*. The original tells the story of the victim of a scientific experiment gone awry, which causes him to shrink to the size of less than an inch. In the original, the shrinking man finds that his pet cat as well as a spider now represent mortal dangers to him.

In Murphy's version, he will be playing those type of situations for laughs.

NEW GENERATION

Behind Murphy, a whole generation of African-American comics, including Chris Rock, Chris Tucker, Dave Chappelle, David Allan Grier, and Katt Williams, are forging their own careers and coming into their own as major stars of film, TV, and standup comedy. Rock and others have acknowledged the influence Murphy has had on their careers. Rock said, according to Bambi Haggins in *Laughing Mad: The Black Comic Persona in Post-Soul America*: "[Murphy] was the first black guy [on the big screen] that I can remember being cool. I can't remember going to see a movie with black people before him."

In fact, Rock owes much of his career success to Murphy, who first saw Rock perform at an "open mic" night at a New York comedy club in 1984. Bowled over with laughter, Murphy helped Rock get some gigs at bigger nightclubs. Later, Rock followed in Murphy's footsteps by winning a role on *Saturday Night Live*. Haggins argued that Murphy's brand of comedy definitely opened doors for Rock and other young African-American comics. She wrote that Murphy is a "model for those who will follow in terms of style [and] content."

Today, many comedians feel a lot more comfortable about trying edgy comedy than they did years ago. Certainly, Murphy was not the first comic to use foul language, or the first comic to soak laughs out of ethnic- and gender-based humor, but Murphy found ways to ratchet up the humor, making audiences nervous until they realized it was all in good fun. By pushing the boundaries of what was regarded as acceptable humor, Eddie Murphy became an American original and his work a flash point in the evolution of comedy.

Selected Filmography

TELEVISION

1980–1984 *Saturday Night Live*

1983 *Eddie Murphy: Delirious*

1987 *Eddie Murphy Raw*

FILM

1982 *48 Hrs.*

1983 *Trading Places*

1984 *Best Defense; Beverly Hills Cop*

1986 *The Golden Child*

1987 *Beverly Hills Cop II*

1988 *Coming to America*

1989 *Harlem Nights*

1990 *Another 48 Hrs.*

1992 *Boomerang; The Distinguished Gentleman*

1994 *Beverly Hills Cop III*

1995 *Vampire in Brooklyn*

1996 *The Nutty Professor*

1998 *Dr. Dolittle*

2000 *Nutty Professor II: The Klumps*

2001 *Shrek; Dr. Dolittle 2*

2002 *Showtime; The Adventures of Pluto Nash; I Spy*

2003 *Daddy Day Care; The Haunted Mansion*

2004 *Shrek 2*

2006 *Dreamgirls*

2007 *Norbit; Shrek the Third*

2008 *Meet Dave*

2009 *Imagine That*

2010 *Shrek Forever After*

1961 Edward Regan Murphy is born in Brooklyn, New York, on April 3.

1964 Murphy's parents divorce; his mother, Lillian, remarries and his stepfather, Vernon Lynch, moves the family to Roosevelt, Long Island.

1976 Murphy performs on stage for the first time, acting as emcee for a talent show at the Roosevelt Youth Center.

1977 The young comic performs professionally for the first time, appearing in comedy clubs on Long Island.

1979 Despite failing many classes and constant truancy due to his comedy career, Murphy graduates high school and starts performing in New York City comedy clubs.

1980 Murphy wins a role as a featured player on *Saturday Night Live*.

1981 Murphy is promoted to a role as a Not Ready for Prime-Time Player on *Saturday Night Live* and develops such popular characters as Gumby, Little Richard Simmons, Buckwheat, and Velvet Jones.

1982 Murphy's first film, *48 Hrs.*, is released to theaters; he plays tough-talking con man Reggie Hammond.

1983 Murphy's second film, *Trading Places*, earns more than $90 million at the box office, establishing the comic as one of the hottest actors in Hollywood.

1984 *Beverly Hills Cop*, which earns more than $300 million at the box office, is released; for the film, Murphy creates the character of streetwise Axel Foley.

1985 Murphy releases his first music CD, *How Could It Be*, featuring the single "Party All the Time," which peaks at No. 2 on the *Billboard* Hot 100 chart.

1988 In the film *Coming to America*, Murphy tries to break away from playing roles as street-smart tough guys; he receives mixed reviews for his acting.

1989 Murphy directs the movie *Harlem Nights*; he also costars in the movie and is skewered by the critics for his acting and direction, while the film's original lead actress, Michael Michele, accuses him of sexual harassment.

1993 Murphy marries model Nicole Mitchell.

1997 After Murphy gives a ride to a prostitute, the actor finds himself at the center of an embarrassing scandal when police stop the car and discover that the prostitute is a man.

1998 Murphy rebounds from the scandal by starring in *Dr. Dolittle*, the first of many family-oriented films he will make over the next several years.

2001 The animated film *Shrek* becomes one of the most popular children's movies of all time, earning some $500 million at the box office; Murphy provides the voice of Donkey.

2002 Murphy stars in what are regarded as the two worst films of his career: *I Spy* and *The Adventures of Pluto Nash*.

2005 Murphy and his wife, Nicole, announce their decision to divorce.

2006 Melanie Brown, a former member of the Spice Girls, says Murphy is the father of their child; a DNA test confirms her assertion.

2007 Murphy wins a Golden Globe Award for his role in *Dreamgirls* and is nominated for an Academy Award for best supporting actor for the film.

2008 Murphy marries film producer Tracey Edmonds in an unofficial ceremony in Bora Bora but soon ends the relationship after Edmonds reportedly refuses to sign a prenuptial agreement.

2009 *Imagine That* is released.

2010 *Shrek Forever After* is released.

Further Reading

Brown, James. *James Brown: The Godfather of Soul*. New York: Thunder's Mouth Press, 1997.

Littleton, Darryl J. *Black Comedians on Black Comedy: How African-Americans Taught Us to Laugh*. New York: Applause Theatre and Cinema Books, 2006.

Miller, Frederic P., Agnes F. Vandome, and John McBrewster, editors. *Eddie Murphy*. Mauritius: Alphascript Publishing, 2009.

Sanello, Frank. *Eddie Murphy: The Life and Times of a Comic on the Edge*. Secaucus, N.J.: Birch Lane Press, 1997.

Shales, Tom, and James Andrew Miller. *Live From New York: An Uncensored History of Saturday Night Live*. Boston: Back Bay, 2003.

Williams, John A., and Dennis A. Williams. *If I Stop, I'll Die: The Comedy and Tragedy of Richard Pryor*. New York: Thunder's Mouth Press, 2006.

WEB SITES

African American Comedy Community
http://www.listofblackcomedians.com

Richard Pryor
http://www.richardpryor.com

Roosevelt, Long Island
http://www.longislandexchange.com/towns/roosevelt.html

Shrek
http://www.shrek.com

Index

Hal Marcovitz is a former newspaper reporter who makes his home in Chalfont, Pennsylvania, with his wife, Gail, and daughter, Ashley. He has written more than 150 books for young readers, including biographies of civil rights leaders Al Sharpton and Eleanor Holmes Norton, farm labor organizer Cesar Chavez, film director Ron Howard, and pop star Madonna. In 2005, his Chelsea House biography of U.S. House Speaker Nancy Pelosi was named to *Booklist* magazine's list of recommended feminist books for young readers.